ROSEMARY VEREY'S GARDEN PLANS

Apples

Artichokes

Box edging

FRANCES LINCOLN
PUBLISHERS

ROSEMARY VEREY'S

Special photography by
Andrew Lawson

Watercolours by
Jean Sturgis

GARDEN PLANS

FRANCES LINCOLN LIMITED
2-4 Torriano Mews, Torriano Avenue,
London NW5 2RZ

British Library Cataloguing-in-Publication Data
A catalogue record for this book is available
from the British Library

ISBN 0-7112-0810-7

Designed and typeset in Janson and Caslon
Swash Italic by Studio Gossett

Printed and bound in Hong Kong
by Wing King Tong Co. Limited

First published by Frances Lincoln Limited:
October 1993

9 8 7 6 5 4 3

HALF-TITLE PAGE: a detail of the plan for the
walled garden at Ascott Place *(see pages 74-79)*

FRONTISPIECE: cottage garden planting in the
Chelsea Flower Show garden *(see pages 58-67)*

RIGHT: white violas in front of *Artemisia*
'Powis Castle', at Hinton House *(see pages 120-123)*

CONTENTS

INTRODUCTION

My garden designing, helped by my husband David, started in a small way, in fact in our own garden where borders, vistas, formal patterns have evolved over thirty years. I loved propagating plants, and soon we had surplus stock that could be sold when the garden was open for the National Gardens Scheme. Visitors asked advice in planning their borders, so I would make a rough sketch on any odd piece of paper, using the plants we had for sale. Then came the question, 'Will you come to our garden to give us some help?'

It was all good fun and I discovered so much – especially about practical gardening; more than I would have learned by going to a gardening school, for every site has its own character. I already had a certain knowledge of and feeling for plants accumulated over the years, an advantage which most students still have to acquire. For hard landscaping I have to rely on contractors, who help me with drainage, levels and technical details.

I uphold Beatrix Farrand's sentiment (Gertrude Jekyll's too), that the design should always fit the site; the site should not be bent to the design. A garden should reflect the character of the owner and the house, not that of the designer. On a first visit I like to listen and to discover as much as I can from the owners. What colours do they like, are they there through the year or away at certain times, will children need their own space, do they enjoy winter gardening, vegetable growing, and many other personal things. I always hope it is not an instant effect the clients are after, for with slow evolvement comes understanding.

It is vitally important that the garden should appear well-designed from the house, so I like to look out from the main windows and doors, then turn back to look at the house again. Taking photographs is important, for reference later. And, at the bottom line – what about finance?

Inevitably designers have their particular style. Mine, I know, is to combine a formal structure with luxuriant planting. First I make a general plan, showing paths, border shapes, prominent features including any major tree-planting. The infilling comes later. I may simply make lists of plants for each area, because I really like to lay the plants out on site. I have a vivid memory of Russell Page working on a large bank in the Pepsi-Cola garden in Upper New York State. He had hundreds of plants in containers, and I watched him placing them with the utmost precision. He was planning on the ground rather than on paper, creating drifts and shapes, giving each plant its correct space. It is a lesson I have never forgotten and I try to do the same whenever possible. This way a plan can be modified, extra plants can be added, reordering can be done if any specimens are of inferior quality, substitutes made when something is not available. If I am working with the gardener I find this is the ideal time to make firm friends with him or her, to discuss colour, the importance of a succession of flowering, and of bringing the garden alive all through the year.

I like to extend the seasons by incorporating lots of early spring bulbs, planting them under deciduous shrubs and through the mixed borders. Summer takes care of itself, but the borders can look tired by autumn, so late-flowering perennials should be included: cimicifugas, anemone hybrids, physostegia, heleniums, rudbeckias, tender lobelias and penstemons.

Difficult moments happen when plants are not available. Nurseries may have sold out of their choicest plants (especially the best roses) by late winter. Although I know it is my own fault if I order too late, it is nevertheless frustrating. I wanted twenty-four standard 'Little White Pet' for the scented garden at Woodside (pages 34-41), but good specimens were not available in

such quantity, so I substituted 'Nozomi'. I was not able to get David Austin's lovely 'Wife of Bath' and 'Pretty Jessica' for the Old Rectory, Berwick (pages 132-9), so we had 'Mary Rose' instead. These are small worries set against the thrill when wonderful specimens arrive.

With a garden, the initial planning and planting is just the beginning. Gardens are always changing and developing. The weather plays a part, of course. Gaps will appear after a hard winter or late spring frosts, and then the fun begins again, as we decide what new treasure to add. Nature does much for you too, and seedlings will sometimes appear at exactly the right place and in the right colour. When my plans are complete and the job is done I like to feel that the garden owners will become confident enough to add their own ideas. Gardening is a continuous learning process. I am constantly finding new plants and through visiting other gardens I discover original ideas and exciting combinations. I hope that I can encourage other gardeners to do the same.

In a planting at Barnsley House, Thalictrum aquilegiifolium, Hesperis matronalis, *fennel and* Helichrysum italicum *make a soft band of colour in front of* Cornus controversa *'Variegata'.*

A TAPESTRY OF COLOUR

THE FOUR PARTERRE beds that frame the lawn on the south-east side of Barnsley House are now more than thirty years old. When I planned them I knew very little about plants and even less about design, but we had grassed over the existing borders, and the day came when we needed more interest and flowers. I had to learn, so I read books, visited gardens and consulted knowledgeable friends.

Looking across bed 4, towards the temple and Magnolia × soulangeana *in bloom. In spring, tulips 'Angélique', 'Mariette' and 'White Triumphator' flower through forget-me-nots and emerging oriental poppies, acanthus and delphiniums. Dark purple lunaria and Bowles' golden grass are strong features.*

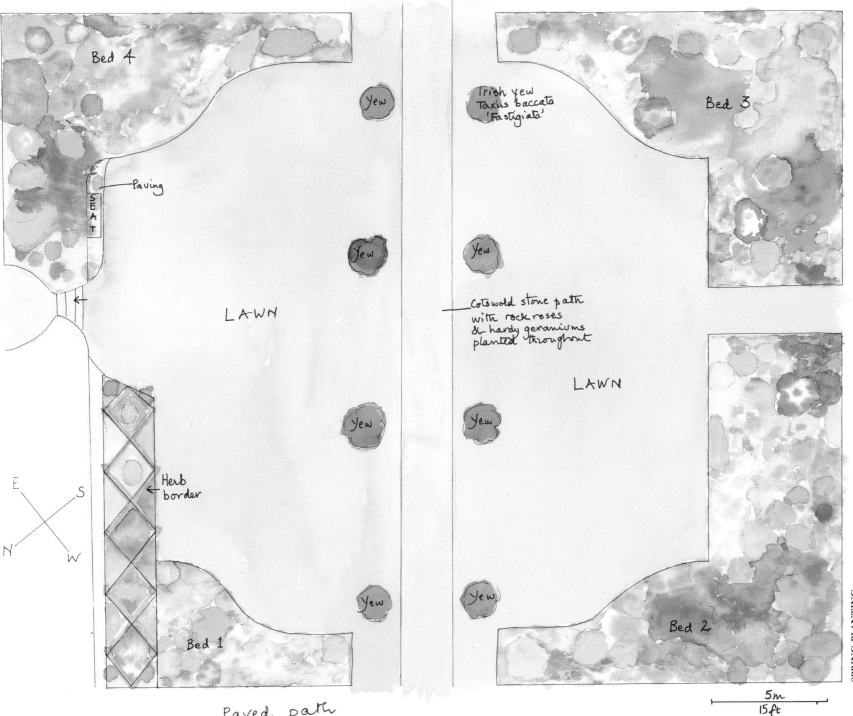

Bed 4

Paving

SEAT

Yew

Irish yew
Taxus baccata
'Fastigiata'

Bed 3

Yew

Yew

LAWN

Cotswold stone path
with rock roses
& hardy geraniums
planted throughout

LAWN

Yew

Yew

E
S
N
W

Herb
border

Yew

Yew

Bed 1

Bed 2

5m
15ft

Paved path

Having read Russell Page's *Education of a Gardener*, I realized that the terrace in front of the house was too narrow. So we made it wider, and at the same time took the opportunity to lay paving to replace the existing gravel, which constantly required weeding. Then we measured the area beyond the terrace and I settled down with pencil and ruler and made shapes to fill the space – and found what fun it was doing this.

I also discovered that the position of the house, the path lined with yew trees and the 1770 stone wall around the garden made it impossible to be too precise. On the ground, so long as you keep a certain symmetry, you do not notice the discrepancies that seem obvious on paper.

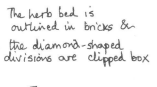

The herb bed is outlined in bricks & the diamond-shaped divisions are clipped box

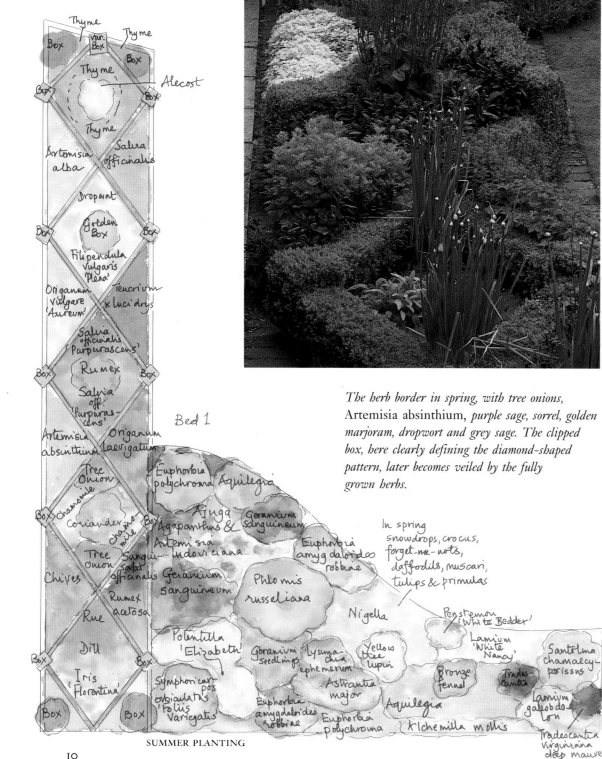

Thyme

Box var. Box Thyme

Box Thyme Box

Alecost

Thyme

Artemisia alba Salvia officinalis

Dropwort

Golden Box

Filipendula vulgaris 'Plena'

Box Box

Origanum vulgare 'Aureum' Teucrium × lucidrys

Salvia officinalis 'Purpurascens'

Box Rumex Box

Salvia off. 'Purpurascens'

Artemisia absinthium Origanum laevigatum

Bed 1

Tree Onion Euphorbia polychroma Aquilegia

Chamomile Ajuga

Box Coriander Box Agapanthus & Geranium sanguineum

Tree Onion Artemisia ludoviciana

Chives Sanguisorba officinalis Geranium sanguineum Euphorbia amygdaloides robbiae

Rumex acetosa Phlomis russeliana

Rue

Dill Nigella Penstemon 'White Bedder'

Iris 'Florentina'

Box Box Potentilla 'Elizabeth' Geranium seedlings Lysimachia ephemerum Yellow tree lupin Lamium 'White Nancy' Santolina chamaecyparissus

Symphoricarpos orbiculatus 'Foliis Variegatis' Astrantia major Bronze fennel Tradescantia

Box Box Euphorbia amygdaloides robbiae Euphorbia polychroma Aquilegia Lamium galeobdolon

Alchemilla mollis

Tradescantia virginiana deep mauve

In spring snowdrops, crocus, forget-me-nots, daffodils, muscari, tulips & primulas

SUMMER PLANTING

The herb border in spring, with tree onions, Artemisia absinthium, *purple sage, sorrel, golden marjoram, dropwort and grey sage. The clipped box, here clearly defining the diamond-shaped pattern, later becomes veiled by the fully grown herbs.*

The important thing is to make a general plan in which vistas and views work, and where there is a satisfying relationship between the different elements. When my shapes became a parterre of four flower beds, two on either side of the yew path, the straight sides of the beds were dictated by the line of the house and the path, while their lawn sides could be gently serpentine.

I was very influenced by the layout of Hidcote (who isn't?), but had decided that while each part of our garden must have its own theme and character, the garden as a whole would not benefit from being divided into such clearly defined 'rooms'. Rather than planting hedges to divide the parterre from the rest of the garden, we would rely for screening on flowering shrubs in the borders. This seemed to work well then, and happily still does. As the shrubs grow we prune them back to size. In summer they provide a pleasing backdrop for flowers, and in winter their branches make an interesting tracery.

The shrubs we have had all this time are *Philadelphus* 'Beauclerk' for scent, *Weigela* 'Bristol Ruby' for colour, *Deutzia scabra* for its flowers, *Berberis* × *ottawensis* 'Superba' for its red leaves in summer, *Cotinus coggygria* for its 'fuzz' and autumn colour. Of the evergreens I originally chose we still have *Osmanthus* × *burkwoodii* for its marvellously scented flowers, *Hebe* 'Mrs Winder' for its foliage and winter flowers and *H. rakaiensis* for its perfect shape (it is the ideal corner shrub). We have also kept *Prunus laurocerasus* 'Zabeliana' and golden privet as infillers and for picking in winter. Since the first planting I have added *Ilex* × *altaclerensis* 'Golden King', *Lavatera* 'Barnsley', *Ceanothus thyrsifolius* var. *repens*, *Hebe topiaria*, *Cytisus battandieri* and *Cornus controversa* 'Variegata'.

The herbaceous and smaller shrub planting was influenced by John and Marjorie Buxton and by Nancy Lindsay. John was for many years in charge of the borders at New College, Oxford, and

Two of the best summer-flowering perennials, Astrantia major, *seen here in its pink form (left, above) and the elegant* Thalictrum aquilegiifolium *(left, below), flourish in bed 2.*

On pages 12-13 The lily-flowered tulip 'China Pink' in bed 3, planted in a bold drift with forget-me-nots. The young rose leaves help to enhance the scene.

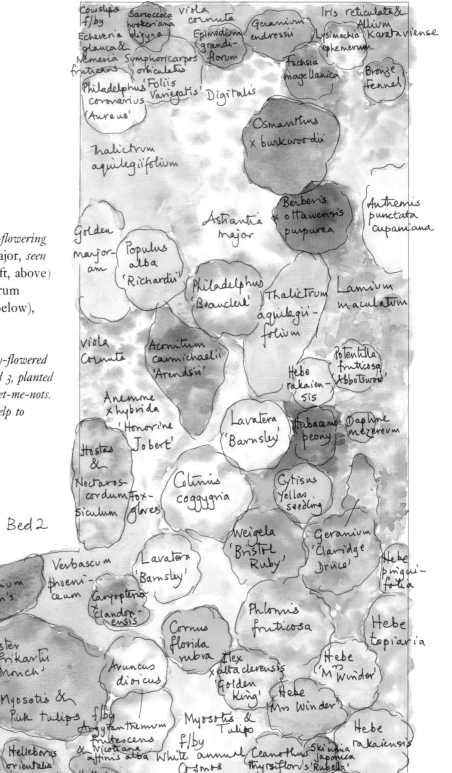

Cowslips f/by
Sarcococca hookeriana
Viola cornuta
Geranium endressii
Iris reticulata & Allium Karataviense
Echeveria glauca & Nemesia fruticans
Epimedium grandi-florum
Lysimachia ephemerum
Symphoricarpos orbiculatus 'Foliis Variegatis'
Fuchsia magellanica
Bronze Fennel
Philadelphus coronarius 'Aureus'
Digitalis
Osmanthus x burkwoodii
Thalictrum aquilegiifolium
Berberis x ottawensis purpurea
Anthemis punctata cupaniana
Golden marjoram
Populus alba 'Richardii'
Astrantia major
Philadelphus 'Beauclerk'
Thalictrum aquilegii-folium
Lamium maculatum
Viola cornuta
Aconitum carmichaelii 'Arendsii'
Hebe rakaien-sis
Potentilla fruticosa 'Abbotswood'
Anemone x hybrida 'Honorine Jobert'
Lavatera 'Barnsley'
Herbaceous peony
Daphne mezereum
Hostas & Nectaroscordum Siculum
Foxgloves
Cotinus coggygria
Cytisus Yellow seedling
Weigela 'Bristol Ruby'
Geranium 'Claridge Druce'
Bed 2
Verbascum phoeniceum
Lavatera 'Barnsley'
Hebe pinguifolia
Geranium 'Johnson's Blue'
Caryopteris x clandonensis
Phlomis fruticosa
Hebe topiaria
Saxifraga hirsuta 'Irish Pride'
Erysimum 'Constant Cheer'
Aster x frikartii 'Mönch'
Cornus florida rubra
Ilex x altaclerensis 'Golden King'
Hebe 'Mrs Winder'
Aruncus dioicus
Hebe 'Mrs Winder'
Spiraea 'Little Princess'
Penstemon rich Purple
Myosotis & Pink tulips f/by Argyranthemum frutescens & Nicotiana affinis alba
Myosotis & Tulips
Hebe rakaiensis
Primulas & crocus f/by Diascia stachyoides
Echium 'Blue Bedder'
Hardy Geranium
Asphodeline lutea
Symphoricarpos orbiculatus 'Foliis variegatus'
Pink tulips & Cistus x Loretii Myosotis f/by Echium 'Blue Bedder'
Blue aquilegias
Helleborus orientalis
Helleborus orientalis
f/by White annual Cosmos
Ceanothus thyrsiflorus repens
Skimmia japonica 'Rubella'
Santolina pinnata neapolitana
Helleborus orientalis
Crocus
Santolina rosmarinifolia
Hebe topiaria
Hebe rakaiensis
Iris reticulata
Alchemilla mollis with Lamium maculatum

Right: *Aquilegias, here seen in bed 3, are allowed to seed themselves through the borders. Flowering in late spring, they bring interest after the tulips and before the main opening of herbaceous perennials. We save seed of some of the best colours, especially pinks and dark mauve, to sow in the seed bed. Centaurea dealbata, in the foreground, flowers for several weeks to complement the columbines.*

Below: *Inspired by a wonderful bed of annual mixed cosmos in a French garden, I now grow Cosmos 'Sensation' in bed 3 each summer. This is the perfect annual to follow on after the tulips and forget-me-nots are taken out. My natural instinct would be to keep to one colour, but sometimes it is good to have a change and we look forward to this rather gaudy display.*

Nancy was an extremely knowledgeable plantswoman who was outstandingly generous with both her plants and her knowledge. She inspired me to use lots of euphorbias and hardy geraniums, mixed with *Phlomis russeliana*, santolinas, *Stachys byzantina*, lamiums and *Alchemilla mollis*. These are all easy plants and, as Nancy said, you can 'use these when you start and more sophisticated varieties as you learn more about your garden'. These 'easy' plants still form the basis of the beds beside the herb border. (This herb border was added as a necessity in 1976. Previously the herbs had all been integrated into the various borders and on days when I had guests for lunch I always seemed to be rushing round the garden at the last minute picking herbs. The herb border, outside what was then my kitchen door, made my life a lot easier.)

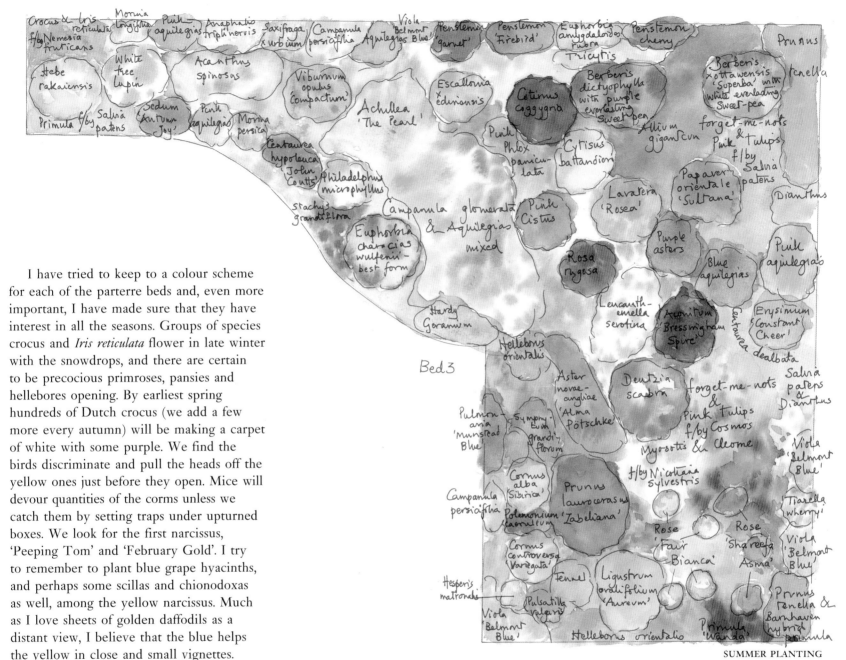

Crocus & Iris reticulata f/by Nemesia fruticans
Morina longifolia
Pink aquilegias
Anaphalis triplinervis
Saxifraga × urbium
Campanula persicifolia
Viola 'Belmont Blue'
Aquilegias 'Blue'
Penstemon 'Garnet'
Penstemon 'Firebird'
Euphorbia amygdaloides rubra
Penstemon cherry
Prunus tenella
Hebe rakaiensis
White tree lupin
Acanthus spinosus
Viburnum opulus 'Compactum'
Tricyrtis
Escallonia × edinensis
Cotinus coggygria
Berberis dictyophylla with purple everlasting sweet-pea
Berberis × ottawensis 'Superba' with white everlasting sweet-pea
Primula f/by Salvia patens
Sedum 'Autumn Joy'
Pink aquilegias
Morina persica
Achillea 'The Pearl'
Pink Phlox paniculata
Cytisus battandieri
Allium giganteum
forget-me-nots Pink & tulips f/by Salvia patens
Centaurea hypoleuca 'John Coutts'
Philadelphus microphyllus
Papaver orientale 'Sultana'
Dianthus
Stachys grandiflora
Campanula glomerata & Aquilegias mixed
Lavatera 'Rosea'
Euphorbia characias wulfenii 'best form'
Pink Cistus
Purple asters
Pink aquilegias
Rosa rugosa
Blue aquilegias
Hardy Geranium
Leucanthemella serotina
Aconitum Bressingham Spire'
Centaurea dealbata
Erysimum 'Constant Cheer'
Helleborus orientalis

Bed 3

Aster novae-angliae 'Alma Pötschke'
Deutzia scabra
forget-me-nots & Pink tulips f/by Cosmos Myosotis & Cleome f/by Nicotiana sylvestris
Salvia patens & Dianthus
Pulmonaria 'Munstead Blue'
Symphytum grandiflorum
Viola 'Belmont Blue'
Cornus alba 'Sibirica'
Prunus laurocerasus 'Zabeliana'
Tiarella wherryi
Viola 'Belmont Blue'
Campanula persicifolia
Polemonium caeruleum
Rose 'Fair Bianca'
Rose 'Sharifa Asma'
Cornus controversa 'Variegata'
Hesperis matronalis
Fennel
Ligustrum ovalifolium 'Aureum'
Prunus tenella & Barnhaven hybrid primula
Viola 'Belmont Blue'
Pulsatilla vulgaris
Helleborus orientalis
Primula 'Wanda'

I have tried to keep to a colour scheme for each of the parterre beds and, even more important, I have made sure that they have interest in all the seasons. Groups of species crocus and *Iris reticulata* flower in late winter with the snowdrops, and there are certain to be precocious primroses, pansies and hellebores opening. By earliest spring hundreds of Dutch crocus (we add a few more every autumn) will be making a carpet of white with some purple. We find the birds discriminate and pull the heads off the yellow ones just before they open. Mice will devour quantities of the corms unless we catch them by setting traps under upturned boxes. We look for the first narcissus, 'Peeping Tom' and 'February Gold'. I try to remember to plant blue grape hyacinths, and perhaps some scillas and chionodoxas as well, among the yellow narcissus. Much as I love sheets of golden daffodils as a distant view, I believe that the blue helps the yellow in close and small vignettes.

By mid-spring the tulips are starting. These are planted through and between the herbaceous plants which by now are sending up luscious young green leaves. Every day brings fresh excitements, and from now until autumn there is no difficulty in ensuring that there is colour in the border to supplement the different greens of the foliage. I always want to maintain the flowering sequence as far as

possible into the autumn, so I'm constantly looking for late flowerers. Recently, and especially since I visited some Irish gardens two autumns ago, we have been increasing our stock of various lobelias, monardas, monkshoods and hemerocallis, and our patch of *Physostegia virginiana* is growing.

Leucanthemella serotina makes a splendid mid-autumn show, and acanthus provides a strong feature, especially good in association with *Anemone japonica*. Perhaps my favourite of all is *Salvia uliginosa*, another recent addition. Its flowers are a soft blue that is rare among autumn colours.

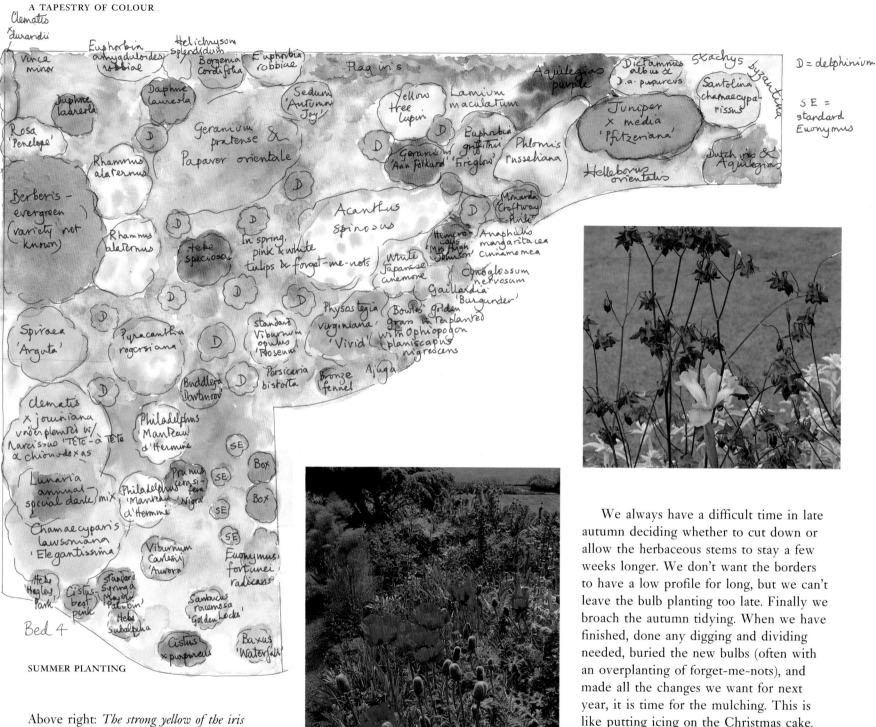

SUMMER PLANTING

Above right: *The strong yellow of the iris holds its own with the equally vivid blue-purple aquilegias. They are both growing through a carpet of* Stachys byzantina, *in a corner of bed 4.*
Right and opposite: *In bed 4, at midsummer, scarlet poppies, blue delphiniums and a glowing yellow tree lupin combine to create an exciting mix of brilliant colours. The bronze iris, added recently, contributes a deeper note.*

We always have a difficult time in late autumn deciding whether to cut down or allow the herbaceous stems to stay a few weeks longer. We don't want the borders to have a low profile for long, but we can't leave the bulb planting too late. Finally we broach the autumn tidying. When we have finished, done any digging and dividing needed, buried the new bulbs (often with an overplanting of forget-me-nots), and made all the changes we want for next year, it is time for the mulching. This is like putting icing on the Christmas cake. We mix leaf mould with well-rotted horse manure, and spread this around quite thickly on the borders. This keeps the soil fertile and with a wonderful workable tilth; not only does it feed the plants, but it adds that final touch that makes people say, 'You are lucky to have such wonderful rich brown soil.' I agree.

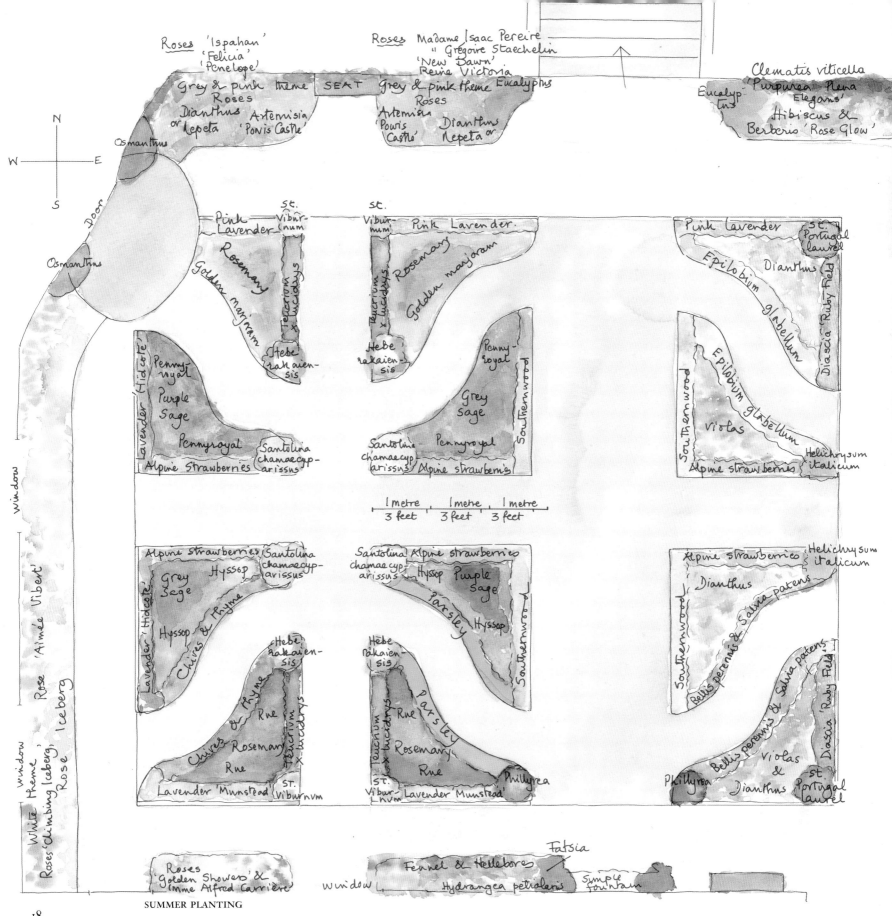

SUMMER PLANTING

AN ENCLOSED HERB GARDEN

Gleditsia triacanthos

Barn

T HE OWNER OF *a sunny farmhouse courtyard invited me to design a herb garden which would be decorative and useful. It would transform the patch outside her kitchen window, which as it existed was just gravel and weeds.*

The space measured 16.5 × 13m (54 × 43ft). It was enclosed on the south and west sides by the house. On the north was a 1.2m (4ft) stone wall with steps, and on the east a barn with an outside staircase leading up to a workshop. On the south-east corner there was a 7m (23ft) wide opening, which let in the wind. This opening was to be closed by a high Cotswold stone wall with a wooden door. The wall, creating an enclosure, would substantially improve the micro-climate, reducing draughts and 'containing the sunshine', which the plants should enjoy.

There were several points to be taken into consideration. There must be an easy way across the garden from the kitchen door to the workshop stairway. The herb beds must be designed for easy access and picking, and should incorporate as many essential herbs as possible. I felt that the design should be symmetrical, and centred on the kitchen window. The barn had a hard surface up to it, but I wanted to have perimeter beds under the other three walls, to take advantage of the three aspects and allow for a diversity of climbers.

For the centre part of the garden I planned eight beds, each in shape a mirror image of the one opposite. As the beds were small, I was able to cut templates of plaster-board to make accurate laying out easier.

Each bed was to be edged with low herbs and filled with taller ones. The

general planting pattern of each would also mirror that of the one opposite, but, for extra interest, there would be differences in planting detail.

The space nearest the workshop could either have four of these eight beds repeated, but with different planting, or be left unplanted (there was mention of a swimming pool to be made there one day).

The final result would be formal in shape but exuberant in planting. I enjoyed drawing up this plan, making the beds fit neatly together with the curving paths between them. The pleasing pattern and the planting for year-round interest and culinary enjoyment make good use of a sheltered area which had never before been fully appreciated.

We all love and cherish the old-fashioned Viola *'Maggie Mott'.*

Epilobium glabellum, *with its delicate white summer flowers, is delightful as an edging plant.*

A FORMAL GARDEN

THE LITTLE HOUSE in Barnsley, Gloucestershire, is guarded from the road by a high beech hedge. This helps to muffle the sound of traffic passing through the village but it is only 3m (10ft) from the façade of the house, so the area between is both narrow and shady. The then owners, Catherine and Arthur Reynolds, wanted to fill this space with interesting planting that would look good at all seasons. Just beyond the path is a small, square area which provides the immediate view from the drawing room doors. Here was the perfect site for a formal garden with a tiny parterre of four flower beds framed by pleached trees.

An early spring view, looking along the narrow vista between the house and the old beech hedge. The planting provides contrast of colour, shape and texture to complement the mellow Cotswold stone. The small parterre – on the left of this picture – is framed on two sides by pleached Sorbus aria 'Lutescens', just bursting into leaf.

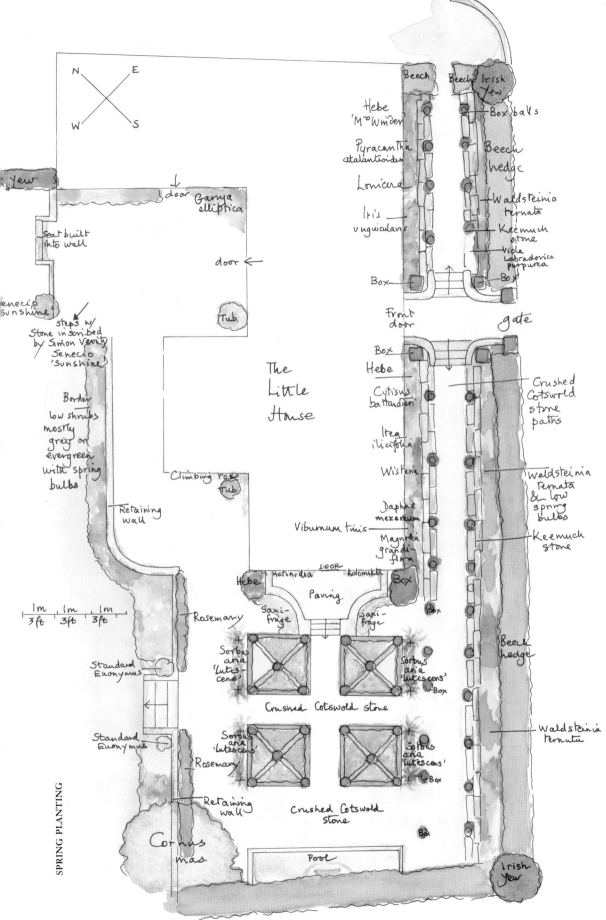

N
E
W
S

Yew

door
Garya
elliptica

Seat built
into wall

Senecio
'sunshine'

steps w/
Stone inscribed
by Simon Verity
Senecio 'sunshine'

Border
low shrubs
mostly
grey or
evergreen
with spring
bulbs

Retaining
wall

1m 1m 1m
3ft 3ft 3ft

Standard
Euonymus

Standard
Euonymus

Rosemary

SPRING PLANTING

Cornus
mas.

Rosemary

Retaining
wall

The
Little
House

Tub.

Climbing rose
tub

Hebe   Actinidia   DOOR   kolomikta
Paving

Saxi-
frage

Saxi-
frage

Sorbus
aria
'Lutes-
cens'

Sorbus
aria
'Lutescens'

Sorbus
aria
'lutescens'

Sorbus
aria
'Lutescens'

Crushed Cotswold stone

Box

Crushed Cotswold
stone

Pool

Hebe
'McWilder'

Pyracantha
atalantioides

Lonicera

Iris
unguicularis

Box

Beech   Beech Irish
Yew

Box balls

Beech
hedge

Waldsteinia
ternata

Keemuch
stone

Viola
Labradorica
purpurea

Box

Front
door

gate

Box

Hebe

Cytisus
battandieri

Itea
ilicifolia

Wisteria

Daphne
mezereum

Viburnum tinus

Magnolia
grandiflora

Box

Crushed
Cotswold
stone paths

Waldsteinia
ternata
& low
spring
bulbs

Keemuch
stone

Box

Beech
hedge

Waldsteinia
ternata

Box

Irish
Yew

THE ENTRANCE

Walk through the front gate, look right and left, and you see planting that is much the same each way. The narrow space running the length of the house and beyond is shaded by the beech hedge. For many months of the year the dominant colour is provided by the tawny brown of beech leaves. I felt that this needed the balance of as much evergreen as possible, so here was an ideal opportunity to use clipped box. We started with a 1.5m (5ft) wide avenue of box balls. These are set alternately with specially cut pieces of Keemuch stone from India, complete with fossils. In addition, a line of the stone runs behind each row of box, acting as an edging to the strips of soil in front of the beech hedge and the house. For the space close to the hedge, where the soil was inevitably poor, I specified a permanent ground cover of the undemanding *Waldsteinia ternata*.

The Little House, now much altered, was originally two Cotswold stone cottages built in the late seventeenth century. The ceilings are low and the outside walls are not high, so we had to confine our choice of climbers to those that can be disciplined. There was an existing, and rampant, early Dutch honeysuckle which could envelop the front door if not restrained. We gave this firm treatment, pruning its side-shoots and tying back the main stems to the wall. At one end of the house wall we planted a yellow-berried pyracantha. As this flowers and fruits on the old wood it is possible to keep it trained tidily to the house. The owners asked for a *Magnolia grandiflora*, and we put it in at the other end. Now, nine years on, it needs to be moved elsewhere before it grows any bigger and encroaches on the roof.

Along the wall we planted an *Itea ilicifolia*, the sweetly scented *Cytisus battandieri* and a wisteria. In front are hebes, a *Daphne mezereum*, and a variegated *Viburnum tinus*. They are all evergreen so keep their good looks in winter.

21

THE PARTERRE

The ground slopes sharply up at the back of the house, and I suspect that three hundred years ago the cottages were built into the side of the hill. This means that the level of the parterre garden is 50cm (20in) higher than the drawing room floor, giving an interesting view from indoors. Instead of looking down on the pattern you are looking along it.

As you can see from the plan, each square is simple, with an outline and diagonals of box. The resulting triangles are small and easy to keep full of quiet colour. The original infillings for four of the triangles were *Viola* 'Belmont Blue' and another four had *V.* 'Mauve Haze'. Both of these flower continuously through spring and summer if you keep them well deadheaded. Another triangle had *Dianthus* 'Loveliness', with a wonderful scent which wafts on the evening air, and an unnamed dianthus occupied another triangle. These sections could have pink dwarf tulips for spring. We reserved four of the other triangles for early bulbs, chionodoxas and more species tulips, followed by *Epilobium glabellum*. In two triangles we experimented with *Lonicera nitida* 'Baggesen's Gold'. These same plants have now been in for nine years and have been clipped regularly, and they are still little yellow platforms only 30cm (12in) high. The violas and dianthus have to be renewed every other year, but both are easy to propagate from cuttings, and different violas can be grown from seed to ring the changes in colour. To give a step-up in height we put in four standard box balls on 75cm (30in) stems, one in the centre of each bed. And we marked each of the sixteen corners with a shapely box pyramid.

Every picture needs a frame. Here, with the beech hedge at one end and the house on the other, it was only the two sides that required framing. I have always been intrigued by 'hedges on stilts'. They give a feeling of structure without being too wall-like and confining. Lime and hornbeam have been used in this way for centuries, and are still the conventional choice, but why not try some other tree? It has to be one that does not resent training and clipping. Prunus and malus are often trained as espaliers and cordons, and they are both members of the Rosaceae family. Following this train of thought, I decided to try their cousin *Sorbus aria* 'Lutescens', and I planted four pleached specimens on each side, leaving a gap for the path between the beds.

When buying trees for this type of hedge it is important to select specimens with branches starting at the same height: in our instance this was at 1.2m (4ft) from ground level. Other branches must be adaptable to being trained sideways at fairly regular intervals. Ours were young trees and all the branches were quite pliable, so we used bamboos as both stakes and horizontals.

As an extra touch, groups of six crown imperials, *Fritillaria imperialis*, were planted around each sorbus, an idea stored in my mind since 1972 when I first saw Peggy Munster's lime walk at Bampton Manor in Oxfordshire. It was carpeted on each side with these dramatic flowers.

We used crushed Cotswold stone for the paths, and this has proved to be such a good thing: it blends far more sympathetically with the stonework of the house and garden than the usual washed gravel. This small parterre garden is peaceful at all times of the day, a restful place to be, or to look out on through the drawing room doors.

Above: *An outline of box provides a firm structure for the parterre. Simon Verity's carved fountain, spouting water into the long pool, contributes sound and movement.*

Opposite: *To the right of the entrance gate, box balls, Keemuch stone, the beech hedge and evergreen pyracantha create an enticing vignette.*

A RAISED FLOWER BED

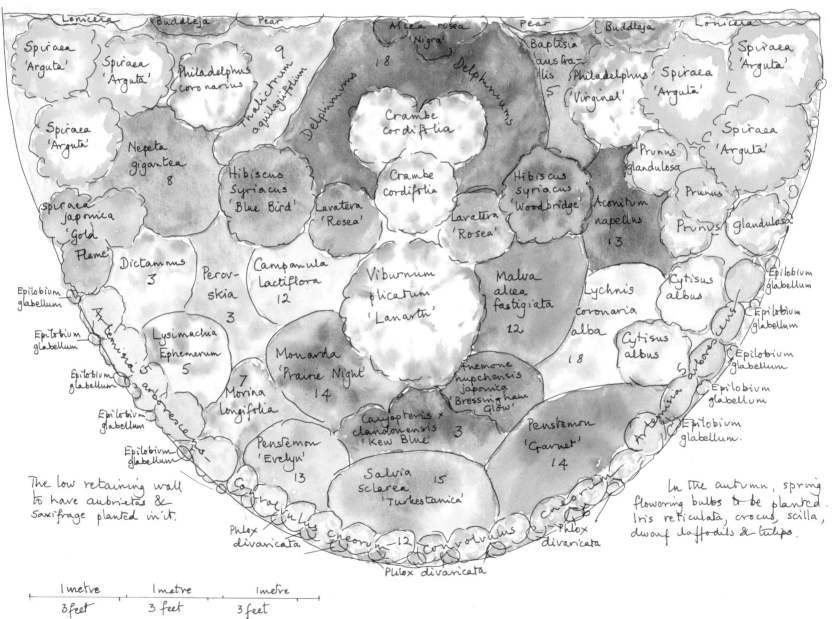

SUMMER PLANTING

N
E
W
S

Lonicera Buddleja Pear Alcea rosea 'Nigra' Pear Buddleja Lonicera

Spiraea 'Arguta'
Spiraea 'Arguta'
Philadelphus coronarius
9
Thalictrum aquilegifolium
18
Delphiniums
Baptisia australis 5
Philadelphus 'Virginal'
Spiraea 'Arguta'
Spiraea 'Arguta'

Spiraea 'Arguta'
Nepeta gigantea 8
Delphiniums
Crambe cordifolia
Prunus glandulosa
Spiraea 'Arguta'

spiraea japonica 'Gold Flame'
Hibiscus Syriacus 'Blue Bird'
Lavatera 'Rosea'
Crambe cordifolia
Lavatera 'Rosea'
Hibiscus syriacus 'Woodbridge'
Aconitum napellus 13
Prunus
Prunus glandulosa

Dictamnus 3
Perovskia 3
Campanula Lactiflora 12
Viburnum plicatum 'Lanarth'
Malva alcea fastigiata 12
Lychnis coronaria alba 18
Cytisus albus
Epilobium glabellum

Epilobium glabellum
Lysimachia Ephemerum 5
Morina longifolia 7
Monarda 'Prairie Night' 14
Anemone hupehensis japonica 'Bressingham Glow'
Cytisus albus
Epilobium glabellum

Epilobium glabellum
Artemisia arborescens
Penstemon 'Evelyn' 13
Caryopteris x clandonensis 'Kew Blue' 3
Penstemon 'Garnet' 14
Epilobium glabellum

Epilobium glabellum
Salvia sclarea 'Turkestanica' 15
Artemisia arborescens
Epilobium glabellum

Epilobium glabellum

The low retaining wall to have aubrietas & saxifrage planted in it.

Convolvulus
Phlox divaricata
Cneorum —12
Convolvulus
Cneorum
Phlox divaricata

Phlox divaricata

In the autumn, spring flowering bulbs to be planted. Iris reticulata, crocus, scilla, dwarf daffodils & tulips.

1 metre	1 metre	1 metre
3 feet	3 feet	3 feet

24

Gardening at Nether Lypiatt in 1886

*S*EVENTEENTH-CENTURY *Nether Lypiatt Manor, in Gloucestershire, is the perfect grand house in miniature, and has attracted many inspired owners. Since 1980, when Prince and Princess Michael of Kent bought the property, the garden has blossomed in a new way. Now there is exciting planting to complement the house and to enhance the mature yew trees, the dramatic lime avenue and the woodland that provides both backdrop and shelter for the garden.*

Above: Hibiscus *'Blue Bird'*, pruned hard in spring, will provide a wonderful show in late summer and autumn.

Above, right: Lavatera *'Rosea'* produces its shocking pink flowers continuously from midsummer until the first frosts.

Princess Michael loves every part of the garden, from the forecourt with its box-edged beds to her rose maze, planted in 1986. Two knot patterns are laid out with shrubby herbs, and the once nettle-ridden path into the woodland is now lined with scented shrubs. In the secret garden beside the house only white and black flowers are allowed.

When we turned our attention to a rather sad area in front of a wall near the rose maze, the Princess suggested that a raised bed should be made. This seemed an excellent plan. A change of level always adds interest to a design. Moreover, in a raised bed tall plants look even taller and often very dramatic, while small flowers at the front, at the top of a low wall, can be enjoyed at closer range.

At Nether Lypiatt the area allocated to the raised bed is 8m (28ft) wide at the back. We decided on a shape that is just more than a semicircle, built up to a height of 75cm (30in).

The planting was carefully planned so that there would be interest for most of the year. Along the back wall are two trained pear trees, two buddlejas and two spring-flowering honeysuckles. In spring *Prunus glandulosa* and *Spiraea* 'Arguta' are in flower, and the young leaves of *S. japonica* 'Gold Flame' create a strong accent. The flowers of *Viburnum plicatum* 'Lanarth' and *Thalictrum aquilegiifolium* soon follow. For the summer months there are bands of colour, with campanulas, nepeta,

delphiniums, mallows and broom, followed by penstemons, lychnis, morina and monarda. A little later, hibiscus, monkshood, perovskia and the skeletons of *Crambe cordifolia* are conspicuous. In the autumn spring-flowering bulbs are planted, to give colour from late winter through until the beginning of summer. It is good policy to mix bulbs in between shrubs and herbaceous plants, which come into their own as the leaves of the bulbs die down.

With its mixed planting, planned for year-round interest, this bed has a different feeling from all the other parts of the garden.

THREE GARDENS

*E*LTON *J*OHN'S GARDEN *at Woodside in Berkshire was an exciting challenge for me, offering the space and the potential for different themes. From the drawing room the owner and his guests can step out into the white garden, where four beds surround a spacious lawn, ideal for entertaining. From here they can stroll beside the long rainbow border. The scented garden is more intimate, with its cooling rill, narrow paths and enclosing trellis.*

A springtime view along the rainbow border, backed by an old hawthorn hedge, with the eighteenth-century orangery in the distance. Beyond the sweeping lawns, the woodland, with many native and exotic trees and shrubs, is developing into a haven for wild life.

Courtyard

House

Scented
garden

oak
tree

White
garden

5
rainbow
beds

E

N   S

W

$\dfrac{5\,m}{15\,ft}$ $\dfrac{5\,m}{15\,ft}$

A SPACIOUS WHITE GARDEN

THE FRENCH WINDOWS of the drawing room at Woodside open on to a stone-paved terrace. The owner decided that this terrace and the area immediately beyond was where he would entertain his friends on summer evenings. A white garden would provide the perfect setting for these summer parties. It would be a peaceful place, a restful interlude among the variety of themes incorporated in the whole garden.

Left: *Spring brings an outburst of bloom in the white garden, with white* Narcissus *'Mount Hood' and N. 'White Lion', a fine variety with inner petals intermingled with soft yellow. The main planting was done in the spring of 1991, and this photograph was taken a year later.* Spiraea *'Arguta', to be seen in the foreground, grew well in the first season, as did* Dicentra spectabilis alba (*pictured* above). *The standard holly,* Ilex *'Argentea Marginata', added in autumn 1991, is especially valuable for winter shape and interest.*

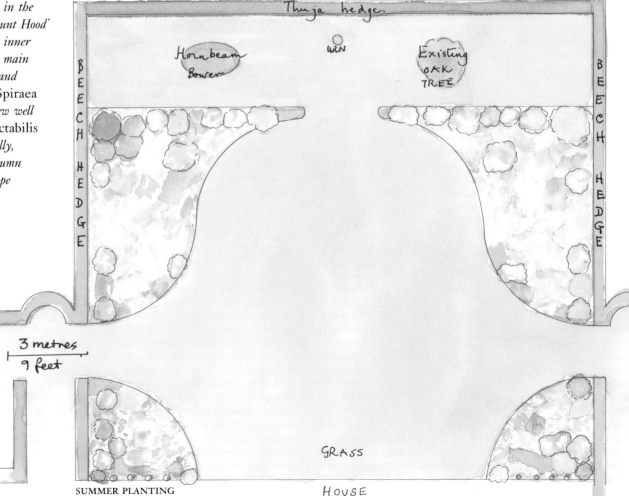

Thuja hedge.

BEECH HEDGE

Hornbeam Bower

urn

Existing OAK TREE

BEECH HEDGE

3 metres
9 feet

GRASS

SUMMER PLANTING

HOUSE

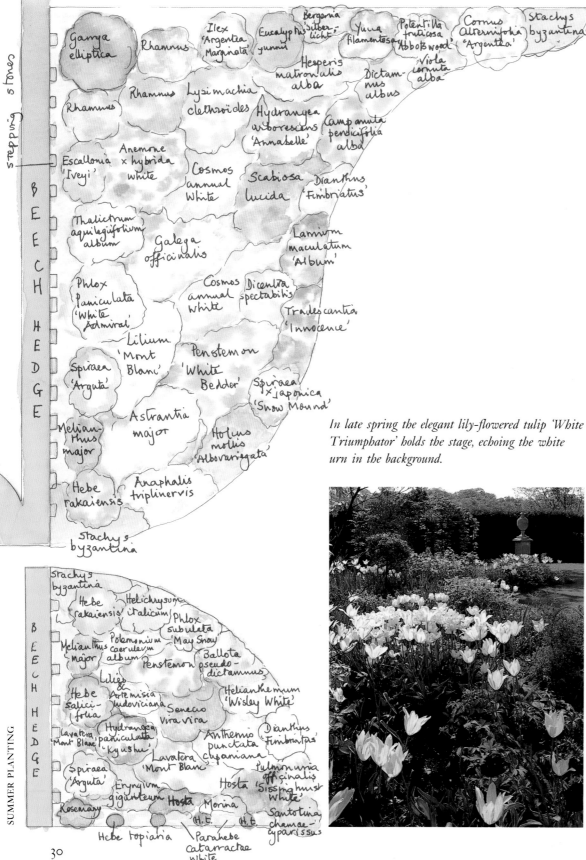

Garden plan labels (top diagram):

stepping stones · corner

BEECH HEDGE

Garrya elliptica · Rhamnus · Ilex 'Argentea Marginata' · Eucalyptus gunnii · Bergenia 'Silberlicht' · Yucca filamentosa · Potentilla fruticosa 'Abbotswood' · Cornus Alternifolia 'Argentea' · Stachys byzantina

Rhamnus · Rhamnus · Lysimachia clethroides · Hesperis matronalis alba · Dictamnus albus · Viola cornuta alba

Escallonia 'Iveyi' · Anemone × hybrida white · Hydrangea arborescens 'Annabelle' · Campanula persicifolia alba

Thalictrum aquilegifolium album · Galega officinalis · Cosmos annual White · Scabiosa lucida · Dianthus 'Fimbriatus'

Phlox paniculata 'White Admiral' · Cosmos annual white · Dicentra spectabilis · Lamium maculatum 'Album' · Tradescantia 'Innocence'

Lilium 'Mont Blanc' · Penstemon 'White Bedder'

Spiraea 'Arguta' · Spiraea × japonica 'Snow Mound'

Astrantia major · Holcus mollis 'Albovariegata'

Melianthus major · Hebe rakaiensis · Anaphalis triplinervis

Stachys byzantina

In late spring the elegant lily-flowered tulip 'White Triumphator' holds the stage, echoing the white urn in the background.

Garden plan labels (bottom diagram):

SUMMER PLANTING · BEECH HEDGE

Stachys byzantina · Hebe rakaiensis · Helichrysum italicum · Phlox subulata 'May Snow'

Melianthus major · Polemonium caeruleum album · Penstemon · Ballota pseudo-dictamnus

Lilies · Hebe salicifolia · Artemisia ludoviciana · Senecio viravira · Helianthemum 'Wisley White'

Hydrangea paniculata 'Kyushu' · Anthemis punctata cupaniana · Dianthus 'Fimbriatus'

Lavatera 'Mont Blanc' · Lavatera 'Mont Blanc' · Pulmonaria officinalis 'Sissinghurst White'

Spiraea 'Arguta' · Eryngium giganteum · Hosta · Hosta · Morina · Santolina chamaecyparissus

Rosemary · H.E. · H.E.

Hebe topiaria · Parahebe catarractae white

The area was bounded by the terrace on the house side and an old thuja hedge opposite. We added beech hedges on the other sides, to enclose an almost square shape.

My co-designers in the overall plan wanted to have a central pool and spectacular fountain, but I resisted this, influenced by the advice of my friend and mentor the late Russell Page. He recommended that as you walk out of a house there should be an open space, of a size carefully related to the size of the garden, space where you can stand, look around and enjoy the planting without feeling overwhelmed. Here, a central lawn would allow guests to circulate freely and appreciate the surrounding borders. To put a fountain in the middle would be like having a large table or sofa in the middle of your drawing room floor at a party.

I started by roughing out the shapes of four beds. These must be symmetrical. Curving lines would provide a satisfying contrast to the overall square shape, and the flowing edges would keep the guests moving easily. At the same time they would make a pleasing pattern when seen from the rooms above, another important consideration, especially as the master bedroom overlooks this part of the garden.

Here are the plants I chose, hoping to give a happy effect from spring through to autumn. For a framework we started by putting at the back, against one of the beech hedges, the beautiful *Populus alba* 'Richardii', a shrub-like poplar with leaves that are golden on top and silver on the underside. We added, on both sides of the garden, *Escallonia* 'Iveyi' and *Spiraea* 'Arguta', and interplanted them with *Phlox paniculata* 'White Admiral', *Crambe cordifolia* and bronze fennel.

As edging I specified two of my favourite low evergreen shrubs, *Hebe topiaria* and the white form of *Parahebe catarractae*. *Hebe* 'Mrs Winder' acts as a good corner plant for two of the beds and is matched on the opposite corners by *H. rakaiensis*. The curved edges are bounded with *Dianthus* 'Chastity' and *D.* 'Fimbriatus', *Helianthemum* 'Wisley White' and *Phlox* 'May Snow'. There are old stand-bys like *Campanula carpatica* f. *alba*, *Anaphalis triplinervis* and *Lamium maculatum* 'Album', and *Pulmonaria officinalis* 'Sissinghurst White'.

The centres of the beds are filled to overflowing with white penstemon (overwintered indoors), white dame's violets, *Astrantia major* and tall grey-leaved cardoons. *Hydrangea arborescens* 'Annabelle' plays an important role in the autumn and so does a clump of *Melianthus major*. There are *Galega officinalis* 'Alba', *Dicentra spectabilis alba* and *Lysimachia clethroïdes*, as well as the white thalictrum with an aquilegia-like leaf.

Grey is always important in a white garden. *Artemisia ludoviciana*, with its soft grey leaves, is one of the best grey plants. *Anthemis punctata* ssp. *cupaniana* flowers for months, forms a wonderful shrub at least 1m (39in) across and will respond quickly to being clipped hard back, putting out new shoots immediately.

White bulbs must not be neglected. So far we have planted narcissus ('Mount

An early spring view, through an arch in the beech hedge. The bulbs were planted in autumn 1991, ready to provide a grand display for the owner the next spring.

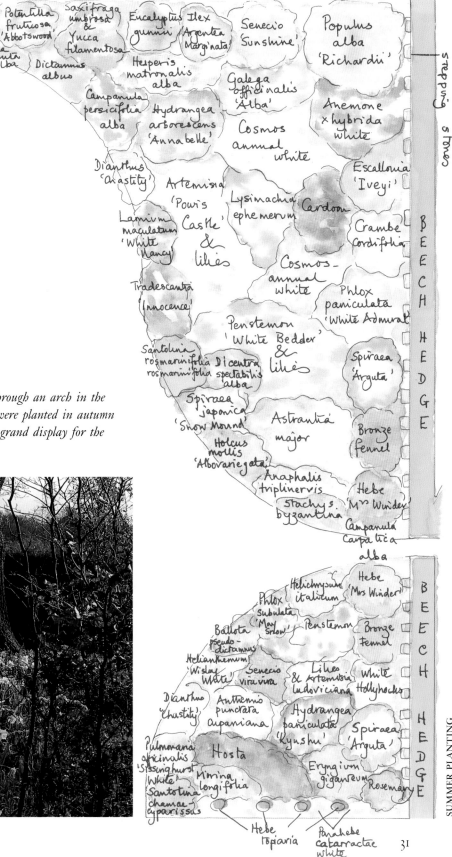

SUMMER PLANTING

31

Hood' and 'White Lion'), the elegant lily-flowered tulip 'White Triumphator', hyacinths and, for later in the year, *Galtonia candicans* and white lilies to appear through the shrubs. Helen Greenwood, the head gardener at Woodside, is assiduous about growing annuals from seed and having them ready to drop into vacant spaces, especially where the bulbs have flowered and been taken out. Maintaining the garden at such a high standard takes constant work and vigilance, but the result is rewarding for both the owner and the gardener.

Designing planting schemes for an owner who only lives in the house at certain times of the year is always a challenge, and especially so when – as often – the client is not fully aware that many plants disappear underground in winter! At Woodside the winter look was going to be particularly important, as the owner would spend some time there at Christmas. Fortunately for me, Helen always co-operates. One day in late autumn we went off together to a local nursery and found two well-shaped 'Argentea Marginata' hollies to put near the two *Eucalyptus gunnii* we had already positioned at the far end of the two larger beds. Then we bought a hundred white cyclamen to drop in between the bulbs and shrubs. They look spectacular with their mottled leaves and ice-white flowers, and they will withstand a slight frost and last for weeks as long as they do not dry out.

In the background, between the borders and the thuja hedge, is an oak tree, probably a hundred years old. To complete the stage set, an oval of hornbeam has been planted nearby and is being trained as an arbour, a living folly with inviting seats. A stone urn nestles between the oak tree and the hornbeam bower, making the focal point from the french windows.

For an extra touch of design interest, Charlie, who does all the clipping so expertly, has started to give the thuja hedge a new look, with swags instead of a flat top, and we are planning to allow some of the

thujas to grow out so that he can make green pillars, or will they be buttresses?

As I listen to my radio I am often delighted to hear Elton John singing – perhaps one day it will be a song about the orange marigold that has found its way into the white garden.

Opposite: *The seedheads and skeleton of Miss Willmott's ghost,* Eryngium giganteum, *harmonize with the upstanding flower heads of* Hydrangea paniculata 'Kyushu'. *In the bed beyond* Anaphalis triplinervis, Astrantia major, Lysimachia clethroïdes *and* Hydrangea 'Annabelle' *make a grand autumn contribution.*

Above: *Annuals and biennials, dropped in where bulbs have faded, keep the beds filled with flowers. The white snapdragons here look fresh and charming throughout the months of summer.* Artemisia ludoviciana *adds a grey accent and* Hosta sieboldiana *bold leaves. The hydrangeas, just beginning to flower, will be all-important in the autumn border.*

Left: *Vita Sackville-West – we are told – dreamed up her white garden while snowflakes were falling. But every white garden must have moments of distraction. Here at Woodside the tulip 'Black Parrot' has found its way among the white flowers – an addition, not an imposition.*

A FRAGRANT OASIS

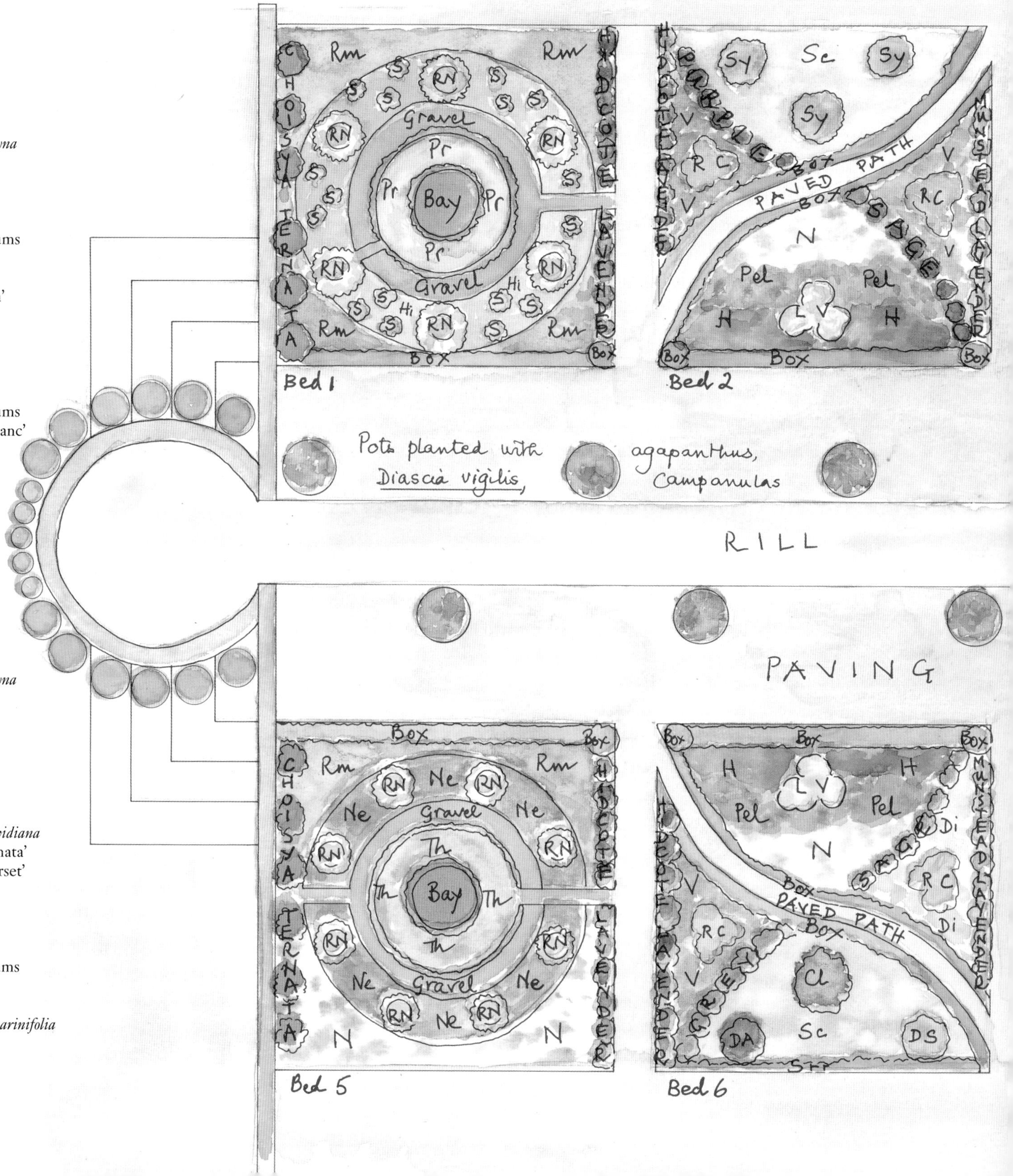

Summer Planting

Bed 1
Hi *Helichrysum italicum*
Pr Pennyroyal
RN Rose 'Nozomi'
Rm Rosemary
S *Sarcococca hookeriana* var. *digyna*

Bed 2
H Heliotrope
LV Lemon verbena
N *Nicotiana sylvestris*
Pel Scented-leaved pelargoniums
RC Rose 'Camaïeux'
Sc *Santolina chamaecyparissus*
Sy *Syringa microphylla* 'Superba'
V Violas

Bed 3
Al *Allium aflatunense*
B *Buddleja davidii* 'Dartmoor'
N *Nicotiana sylvestris*
Pel Scented-leaved pelargoniums
PhBB *Philadelphus* 'Bouquet Blanc'
RC Rose 'Camaïeux'
Sc *Santolina chamecyparissus*
V Violas
Vb *Viburnum × burkwoodii*

Bed 4
G *Genista aetnensis*
Hi *Helichrysum italicum*
Hm *Hamamelis mollis*
M Matthiola
Pi Pittosporum
Pr Pennyroyal
RN Rose 'Nozomi'
S *Sarcococca hookeriana* var. *digyna*

Bed 5
N *Nicotiana sylvestris*
Ne Nepeta
RN Rose 'Nozomi'
Rm Rosemary
Th Thyme

Bed 6
Cl *Clematis heracleifolia* var. *davidiana*
DA *Daphne odora* 'Aureomarginata'
DS *Daphne × burkwoodii* 'Somerset'
Di Dianthus
H Heliotrope
LV Lemon verbena
N *Nicotiana sylvestris*
Pel Scented-leaved pelargoniums
RC Rose 'Camaïeux'
Sc *Santolina chamaecyparissus*
Srr *Santolina rosmarinifolia rosmarinifolia*
V Violas

Bed 1

Bed 2

Pots planted with Diascia vigilis, agapanthus, Campanulas

RILL

PAVING

Bed 5

Bed 6

Bed 3

Bed 4

Bed 7

Bed 8

YOU MAY CARRY *a garden picture in your mind for years, until you finally come across the exact site for the idea. The first instant I entered the front door at Woodside and realized it was possible to see straight through the house into the garden beyond, I knew that this was the place for a rill creating a continuous vista with arching water jets, inspired by the famous fountain canal at the Generalife in Granada. The concept of surrounding the rill with a scented garden enclosed by trelliswork came later.*

BED 7
Al *Allium aflatunense*
B *Buddleja davidii* 'Dartmoor'
Di Dianthus
N *Nicotiana sylvestris*
Pel Scented-leaved pelargoniums
PhA *Philadelphus* 'Avalanche'
RC Rose 'Camaïeux'
Sn *Santolina pinnata* ssp. *neapolitana*
Srr *Santolina rosmarinifolia rosmarinifolia*
V Violas
Vb *Viburnum × burkwoodii*
BED 8
G *Genista aetnensis*
Hm *Hamamelis mollis*
N *Nicotiana sylvestris*
Ne Nepeta
Pi Pittosporum
Ro *Reseda odorata*
RN Rose 'Nozomi'
Th Thyme

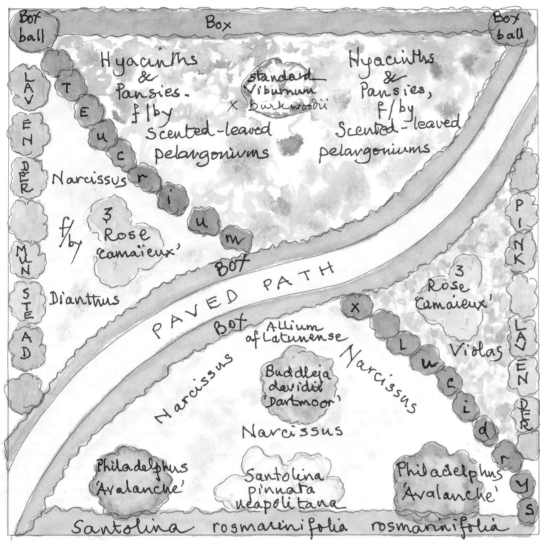

Box ball • Box • Box ball

LAVENDER

Hyacinths & Pansies. f/by Scented-leaved pelargoniums

standard Viburnum x burkwoodii

Hyacinths & Pansies, f/by Scented-leaved pelargoniums

TEUCRIUM

Narcissus

f/by 3 Rose 'Camaieux'

Box

PAVED PATH

Box

Dianthus

MUNSTEAD

Narcissus

Allium afLatunense

Buddleja davidii 'Dartmoor'

Narcissus

Narcissus

X LUCIDRYS

Violas

3 Rose 'Camaieux'

PINK LAVENDER

Philadelphus 'Avalanche'

Santolina pinnata neapolitana

Philadelphus 'Avalanche'

Santolina rosmarinifolia rosmarinifolia

BED 7, SPRING PLANTING

Overlooked as it is from the house, this garden needs a strong design. Fortunately, there is no mathematical problem. With the rill running down the centre and stone paths each side of it, I was able to plan eight equal square beds. The axis of the rill is emphasized by box edging and clipped box balls, and there are lavender-lined paths between the beds.

I planned the four central beds and the four end ones with quite different rhythms in mind. In the centre beds the narrow paths, edged with box, are designed to wander from one corner to another and from one bed to its neighbour. The paths are crossed by ribbons of aromatic herbs – wall germander in two of the beds, sage in the other two – and each of the divisions created is to be filled with scented shrubs with equally fragrant underplanting. Every year the plants can be different, ringing the changes with spring forget-me-nots, narcissus, pansies, wallflowers, hyacinths or polyanthus, followed by nicotiana, scented-leaved pelargoniums, mignonette or heliotrope.

I gave the four end beds a circular pattern, with paths running through so that you can walk right round and savour the scent of each plant on your way. (Originally I planned that the paths should be gravel, but as we laid the garden out we decided that brick would be better.) As you stroll around each inner circle, you are greeted, at head height, by the fragrant flowers of standard roses 'Nozomi'. They are underplanted with *Nepeta mussinii* in two squares and sarcococca in the other two.

A tallish central feature was needed, and four twisted-stem bay trees, 1.5m (5ft) tall, exactly fitted the situation. Each is ringed by a circle of clipped box surrounded with herbs (thyme in two of the squares and pennyroyal in the other two). Some corners are planted with rosemary, others with

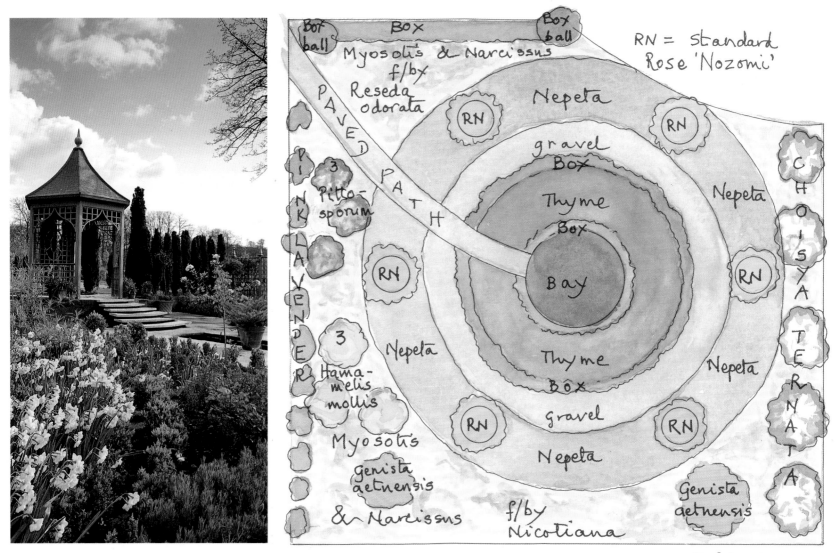

The diagram of Bed 8, spring planting, contains the following labels:

Box ball · BOX · Box ball

RN = standard Rose 'Nozomi'

Myosotis & Narcissus f/by Reseda odorata

PAVED PATH

PINK LAVENDER

3 Pittosporum

3 Hamamelis mollis

Myosotis

Genista aetnensis

& Narcissus

f/by Nicotiana

Nepeta · RN · RN

gravel Box

Thyme

Box

Bay

Thyme

Box

gravel

Nepeta

CHOISYA TERNATA

Nepeta · RN

Nepeta

Genista aetnensis

RN · RN · RN

BED 8, SPRING PLANTING

Above, left: *In bed 7, standard* Viburnum × burkwoodii *was surrounded the first spring by a mass of blue hyacinth 'Bismarck' interplanted with pansies.*

Above: *A spring view across the rill garden, with* Narcissus *'Cheerfulness' in the foreground.*

Right: *The rill garden in summer. The pelargoniums have almost outgrown their allotted space between the soft pink rose 'Heritage' and too-bright 'Cameo'. 'Heritage' was added to the planting later, and fits in well. 'Cameo', however, was planted by mistake – the Gallica rose 'Camaïeux' was what I intended!*

pittosporum, genista and hamamelis. Until these shrubs grow larger the spaces between must be filled by forget-me-nots and many spring bulbs.

My chief challenge in choosing plants was to provide scent all through the year. Some scents waft to you on the air – the perfume of lilies and roses is like this. Other flowers only release their true scent when you can smell them closely. The scents of leaves are often most appreciated as you brush against them, or pick a leaf and squeeze it between your fingers. This is true of rosemary and many of the pelargoniums.

For midwinter we have to rely on the foliage scents of choisya, lavender, thymes, rosemary, pennyroyal and the curry plant, *Helichrysum italicum.* In late winter and early spring the small flowers of the sweet box, *Sarcococca hookeriana* var. *digyna*, open to waft their strong, honey-like scent on the air.

There are fragrant viburnums for every month through winter and spring. I chose *Viburnum × burkwoodii*, because this deliciously fragrant variety grows well as standards, which add height.

Inevitably one selects one's favourites among the wealth of shrubs with scented flowers. I left out wintersweet and flowering honeysuckle – though wonderful flowering shrubs they have undistinguished foliage and would occupy too much valuable space in summertime. They are planted elsewhere in the garden.

The scent of the daphnes wafts strongly on the air. The two I have chosen flower at different times. The evergreen *Daphne odora* 'Aureomarginata' makes a bush about 1m (39in) high; the deep pink to purple flower clusters open in early spring. In late spring and early summer the air is scented by the softer pink flowers of *D. × burkwoodii*.

Handsome, well-filled clay pots embellish the austere pale stone paving on either side of the rill, while also helping to mask the metal water jets. In summer they are filled with agapanthus, Diascia vigilis *and annual campanulas.*

Summer is easily taken care of with roses, pinks and tobacco plants, as well as a variety of scented pelargoniums. I added two of the smaller cultivars of mock orange, *Philadelphus* 'Avalanche', a semi-erect shrub with smallish leaves and rather slender branches, and *P.* 'Bouquet Blanc', with double flowers. They both bloom at midsummer and their leaves are more delicate than the more frequently grown *P. coronarius* and *P.* 'Belle Etoile'.

My chosen lilac is another elegant shrub. *Syringa microphylla* 'Superba' is a plant which draws attention to itself, with small pointed leaves and handsome panicles of fragrant rosy pink to pale mauve flowers in midsummer. It will often bloom again, but in less profusion, in early autumn, and continue until frost. This small-leaved lilac

is useful as a standard shrub, especially where space is limited. I also grow it in a large container, in my own garden.

Among the scented autumn shrubs, my choice is *Buddleja davidii* 'Dartmoor', which takes over after the philadelphus have finished flowering. This buddleja, with its great attraction for bees and butterflies, puts out huge, much-branched panicles of soft mauve blooms just when the *Teucrium* × *lucidrys* is in flower. The two plants make an interesting combination, for they harmonize in one way, and contrast in others. Their flowers are much the same colour, but whereas the long buddleja branches sweep gracefully down with the weight of the blossom, the stems of the wall germander, only 50cm (20in) high, are held upright. The narrow leaves of the

buddleja are matt and grey and those of the germander dark green and shining.

The first year we didn't have the wallflowers or polyanthus – these will be grown on from seed in succeeding years. But in the rich new soil which these beds had been given, the narcissus, hyacinths and winter pansies did brilliantly, and the scented pelargoniums and *Nicotiana sylvestris* got quite carried away. The nicotiana grew to 2.5m (8ft) and more, were reduced to half their height and then produced candelabra shapes, equally tall – the evening scent was potent. The pelargoniums made exuberant growth and outsize foliage, luscious and fragrant. The heliotrope – with its cherry-pie scent, one of my top favourites – responded generously, too.

This garden will always be quite labour-intensive, with the clipping of the box edging and the changing from winter and spring bedding to the summer flowers. It should always look full, and within its formal layout must have a feeling of luxuriance and generous planting.

In winter and early spring the pots beside the rill hold the evergreen Lonicera pileata *with its spreading horizontal branches* (left, below). *Later they will don their colourful summer attire of agapanthus, diascia and campanulas* (left, above, and pages 38-9). *Ferns are kept ready to fill any seasonal gap.*

Right: *As you come out of the garden door, your eye is led past the pond surrounded by box balls and pyramids, along the ever-moving water in the rill to the gothic-style gazebo, framed by tall yews. The sound of splashing water creates a feeling of coolness and calm and offers immediate enticement to enter the garden.*

A RAINBOW BORDER

Above: *In bed 3 the clear blue flowers of* Salvia uliginosa *harmonize with the different blues of* Aster × frikartii *and* Eryngium tripartitum.

Opposite: *The predominant colours of bed 3, at the centre of the border, are blue, pale mauve, cream and grey.* Agastache urticifolia *'Alba' flowers generously for weeks in summer, its height and mass concealing the diagonal dividing path.* Nepeta mussinii, Hosta *'Royal Standard' and white violas fill the corners of the bed.*

*T*HE LONG HAWTHORN *hedge which divides the garden at Woodside from the neighbouring field provided the ideal background for a well-planted mixed border. It was important that the border should be full of interest throughout the year, with a strong basis of evergreen and shapely shrubs to maintain its attraction in winter.*

An uninterrupted 50m (55 yard) border is too long for convenience: a border of this length has to have paths so that there is access from front to back without having to walk – or push a wheelbarrow – right round. However, I wished this border to appear continuous. My solution was to divide it into five sections with grass paths running diagonally between them. These paths are not apparent as you look from end to end – you only become conscious of them as you walk beside them.

Each of the five beds has a different colour scheme. I decided that we would reverse Gertrude Jekyll's principle of starting with grey and white and moving through pinks, blues and mauves to hot colours in the middle of the border. Here we would plan for the hot, bright colours – reds, oranges and yellows – to be at each end, in the beds nearest to the house and furthest from it, while the central, largest bed would be filled with soft blues, off-white and grey; always remembering that green will be the predominant colour throughout the year. All the beds have their framework of shrubs, which gives a feeling of permanence and solidity, especially in winter.

My chief reason for placing the cool colours in the centre was that I wanted this border to feel close to the house, easily within the scope of a stroll before or after dinner. Hot, bright colours stand out and appear closer to you, while cool blues and greys recede and seem further away. If the greys and blues were in the furthest bed they could easily appear to recede into the distance – too far away to walk to and enjoy.

The front of each bed has its own curved shape, in contrast to the straight line of the hedge at the back. I drew these shapes out very roughly on paper, making the middle bed both longer and wider than the others. The lines of the diagonal paths were best decided on the ground. We experimented using bamboos and twine, my aim being to make them one mower's width, and as little obvious as possible.

A great deal of hard work went into the preparation of the soil. The beds were thoroughly double-dug and liberally dosed with farmyard manure and mushroom compost, then allowed to settle before being planted. The result was a good, friable soil, easy to work, and all the plants got off to a good start.

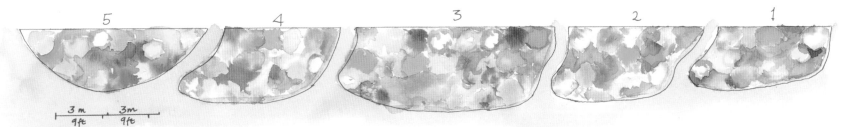

5   4   3   2   1

3 m / 9ft   3 m / 9ft

Above: *In bed 1 golden flowers and foliage mix
and contrast with rich purple-bronze leaves. In
spring there are drifts of tulips 'Yellow Present'
and 'Fringed Elegance' beside* Heuchera *'Palace
Purple'. The golden bracts of* Euphorbia
palustris *echo the yellow pea flowers on the
standard* Caragana arborescens. *Behind are*
Spiraea × vanhouttei *and berberis.*

Right: *Continuing the theme, the shining wide
leaves of* Plantago major rubrifolia *contrast
with the soft foliage of golden lamium.*

Opposite: *Beds 3, 4 and 5 are dominated in
spring by the brilliant tulips 'Golden Harvest',
'Christmas Gold', 'Generaal de Wet', 'Yellow
Dover' and 'Sunkist'.*

As I have no computer which I can turn to and which will immediately flash up all the bright red or orange flowers, I have to do my choosing the long way, going through catalogues and my own old notes, marking the colours and types of plants which will suit my plan, the soil, and, most important of all, the inclinations and personal taste of the owner. In this case he told me that he loved the flowers he remembered from his boyhood, delphiniums, hollyhocks, peonies, lupins, exactly my own choice for my garden at home. This was a good start.

The next task was to calculate approximately how many perennials would be needed. We worked out that the total area of the border was 225 square metres (270 square yards). After taking off 20 square metres (24 square yards) for the grass paths and another 50 square metres (60 square yards) for the space that shrubs would occupy at the back, I was left with 155 square metres (186 square yards). Using 10 plants to the square metre I would need roughly 1550 plants. Some would come from my own garden, and maybe I would be able to buy the rest wholesale from a single nursery (always an economy).

In the end this was what we did. 710 good and well-packed plants came direct from a wholesale nursery. They were delivered in one consignment and mostly bare-rooted, on a day in late spring. I brought a further 510 plants from Barnsley four days later, arriving early with my two gardeners, Andy and Les.

At Woodside, Helen, the head gardener, had everything prepared as far as possible, with the nursery plants already standing beside their intended borders. While my van and car were being unloaded she and I stood the viburnums and yuccas at the front corners of each of the beds, strategically placed where they would eventually mask the grass paths. While Andy and Les were planting these, Helen and I carefully placed the perennials. I tried to get every bed

Bed 5

Spiraea x vanhouttei
Berberis
Viburnum 'Pragense'
Garrya elliptica
Helianthella quinquenervis
Ricinus
Spiraea x vanhouttei
Caragana arborescens 'Pendula'
Euphorbia palustris
Papaver 'Scarlet King'
Caragana arborescens 'Pendula'
Aster novae-angliae 'Andenken an Alma Pötschke'
Aster novi-belgii 'Red Sunset'
Penstemon 'Rich Purple'
Caragana arborescens 'Pendula'
Paeonia lactiflora 'L'Etincelante'
Bergenia 'Sunningdale'
Yucca
Paeonia lactiflora 'Alexander Fleming'
Solidago 'Golden Thumb'
Nicotiana langsdorfii
Coreopsis verticillata 'Moonbeam'
Paeonia lactiflora 'Felix Crousse'
Papaver 'Rembrandt'
Asphodeline lutea
Plantago major rubrifolia
Viola 'Prince John'
Oenothera tetragona 'Fireworks'
Penstemon 'Firebird'
Sedum 'Autumn Joy'
Schizostylis coccinea
Helianthemum 'Cherry Red'
golden Lamium
Penstemon 'Firebird'

SUMMER PLANTING

Bright colours were planned for bed 5, to make an impact in the distance. Euphorbia palustris (left) *is backed by* Ricinus communis *'Impala'* (below, left). *This castor oil plant, though woody, is best treated as an annual, the seed sown in late winter. It will reach 1.8m (6ft). The annual* Rudbeckia *'Marmalade'* (below, right), *planted in bed 1, is a favourite of mine for its striking flowers, excellent for cutting.*

systematically laid out before the planting started. There is no advantage in hurrying at this stage. It is much better to spend time getting each plant as far as possible in the right position to start with than to rely on making alterations later.

We purposely left space to be filled with penstemons, diascias, verbenas and the annuals which Helen had been growing from seed. With some extra plants I brought over a couple of weeks later the total reached 1600, so the estimate was not far out.

Inevitably there were changes and additions to the original plans. For extra height in the first and end beds (1 and 5) we

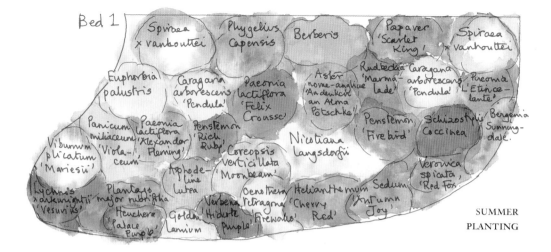

Bed 1

Spiraea × vanhouttei — Phygelius capensis — Berberis — Papaver 'Scarlet King' — Spiraea × vanhouttei

Euphorbia palustris — Caragana arborescens 'Pendula' — Paeonia lactiflora 'Felix Crousse' — Aster novae-angliae 'Andenken an Alma Pötschke' — Rudbeckia 'Marmalade' — Caragana arborescens 'Pendula' — Paeonia 'L'Etincelante'

Viburnum plicatum 'Mariesii' — Panicum miliaceum 'Violaceum' — Paeonia lactiflora 'Alexander Fleming' — Penstemon 'Rich Ruby' — Coreopsis verticillata 'Moonbeam' — Nicotiana langsdorfii — Penstemon 'Firebird' — Schizostylis coccinea — Bergenia 'Sunningdale'

Lychnis × arkwrightii 'Vesuvius' — Plantago major rubrifolia — Heuchera 'Palace Purple' — Asphodeline lutea — Golden Lamium — Verbena 'Hidcote Purple' — Oenothera tetragona 'Fireworks' — Helianthemum 'Cherry Red' — Sedum 'Autumn Joy' — Veronica spicata 'Red Fox'

SUMMER
PLANTING

added standard weeping caraganas. We had originally planned to include *Papaver* 'Oriana', but it proved to be too violent an orange. We added *Heuchera* 'Palace Purple' and the purple form of plantago to the planting at the front of the beds. *Phygelius capensis*, ricinus and *Panicum miliaceum* 'Violaceum' were all added further back. In autumn we planted huge blocks of yellow tulips and cowslips. Of the planting in these beds we were particularly pleased with *Euphorbia palustris* and coreopsis, which were wonderful value for long-lasting effect, and *Schizostylis coccinea*, which flowered till late autumn.

These four plants, all used in beds 1 and 5, make a strong impact. Sedum *'Autumn Joy'* (right) *comes into its own in late summer, attracting scores of butterflies. Another late flowerer is* Schizostylis coccinea *(below, left), a South African bulb, hardier than its looks imply. The clump-forming* Asphodeline lutea *(below, centre) has strap-like evergreen leaves. The flowers open in succession along the strong 1m (39in) stems. A wonderful infiller for summer,* Nicotiana langsdorfii *(below, right) has lime-yellow flowers with a blue eye and blue stamens.*

In beds 2 and 4 the prevailing colours are blue-reds with pinks and white. Lythrum 'The Rocket' reflects the hint of red in Astrantia major. Annual Anoda cristata 'Opal Cup' is added when the peonies fade.

The theme in bed 2 is pink and grey, so there are peonies, *Verbena* 'Silver Anne', *Lythrum* 'The Rocket' and plenty of diascias. The peonies and poppies make brief but beautiful surprises and both *Lavatera* 'Barnsley' and *L.* 'Rosea' provide a continuous show through summer and well into autumn. The annuals in this bed are *Antirrhinum* 'Liberty Lavender', *Anoda cristata* 'Opal Cup' and *Maurandya erubescens*. This last was a great success. It fairly romped away, first trained over pea sticks, then covering peonies and almost smothering the rampant *Lavatera* 'Barnsley'.

The centre bed (3), of blues and mauves, which I thought would be easiest of all, has not always pleased us. There were never enough true blue plants. The spectacular *Buddleja davidii* 'Dartmoor' has done magnificently, and the eryngiums with their metallic blue heads make a fine display.

SUMMER PLANTING

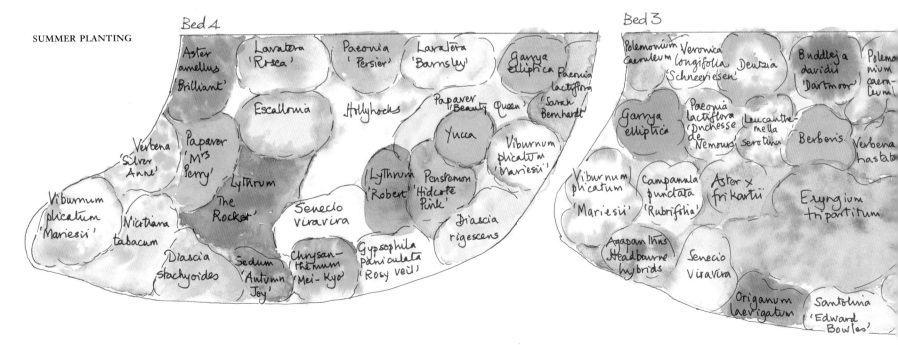

The planting of the next bed (4) is almost a reflection of that in bed 2, but there are bold groups of hollyhocks and the pink *Nicotiana tabacum*, which grew to 1.5m (5ft) and had huge leaves all ready to dry for smoking in a pipe.

It is hard to forgive the rabbits for the havoc they created in this border in the first two years. They attacked a surprising range of plants – campanulas, gypsophila, sedums, *Chrysanthemum* 'Mei-Kyo'. But I suppose like humans they have a variety of favourite tastes, their menus changing according to the season and tenderness of new growth.

Borders never stay still. They must always be improved, even after only two years. Helen and I are planning bluer and better flowers for the central part of this border. Now that the rabbit fencing has been put up we hope that future plants will be able to avoid rabbit stress. As with any garden, maintenance and improvement present a constant challenge, and although much of gardening is in the mind of the creator, the fulfilment is in the eye of the beholder.

The fully double Paeonia lactiflora *'Sarah Bernhardt', planted in beds 2 and 4, has incomparably beautiful flowers, with a faint scent. The young shoots are a rich crimson.*

At the centre of bed 3, the flower heads of Eryngium tripartitum *change gradually from green to purple, until they match their alluring stems.*

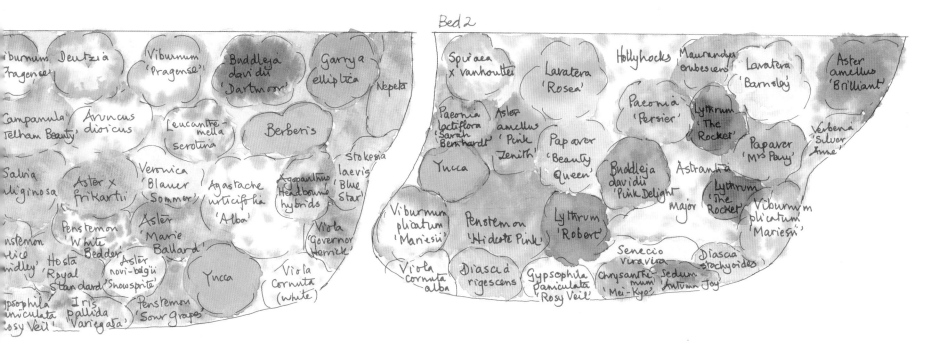

Bed 2

A HERB, BEE AND BUTTERFLY GARDEN

I WAS DELIGHTED to receive, in my post one morning, a cutting from the Montreal Gazetteer. *It was an article by Stuart Robertson, saying, 'The herb garden is an absolute jewel this year. If you have ever thought of planning your own herb garden, give this one a good look over. Not only is the selection worth seeing, but the combination of foliage colours and shapes is harmonious.'*

My herb garden for the Montreal International Floralies 1980 came about in rather unusual circumstances. In December 1979 I had a call from Dick Balfour, President of the Royal National Rose Society, asking if he could come and see me. On 23 December, amidst a family party, he explained his dilemma. Several British organizations, including the Royal Horticultural Society, had been approached by the organizers of the Montreal Floralies, with a request that they should coordinate a British garden for the 1980 show, due to open at the end of May. All had declined. Unhappy that there would be no British representation, Dick had undertaken to organize a garden himself, and was now seeking help from various nurseries and individuals.

Pierre Bourque, chief horticulturist of the Floralies and of the Montreal Botanic Garden, generously agreed that, if plants and transport were provided, the Botanic Garden staff would take responsibility for planting in 1980 and care in subsequent years, when the site would become a permanent garden. The British garden was on, with no time to spare.

The huge site allocated to the garden (3,500 square metres/4,186 square yards) was divided into clearly defined planting areas. Bill Blackburn of Pennine Nurseries drew up the planting plans for perennials and some shrub beds, Peter Harkness designed the beds of modern roses, Dick those for shrub roses, and Peter Lucas Phillips provided the basic design for the cottage garden. Beth Chatto agreed to donate plants for the woodland garden, Pennine Nurseries to give perennials and shrubs, Thompson and Morgan, Suttons, and Hurst to supply seeds. Haddonstone gave a sundial and Charles Verey a seat. The Historic Houses Association offered to sponsor beds, and Manchester Liners provided, free of charge, a large container to ship the plants to Montreal.

My contribution was the herb garden, designed in conjunction with Dick's bee and butterfly garden. Dick and I decided to divide our joint site (a square of roughly 8m/28ft) down the centre, and to place the Haddonstone sundial in the middle. We would have a 1.5m (5ft) path running between the two halves. On one side Dick would design a garden for his bee and butterfly plants, and I would plan and donate the herbs for the other side.

In specifying the planting, I included

Basil, a beautiful herb, and an essential for anyone interested in cooking. Grow annually from seed.

both culinary and aromatic-leaved herbs – the curry plant, *Helichrysum italicum*, southernwood, *Artemisia abrotanum*, and bergamot. Annuals and biennials, parsley, chervil, borage and marigolds – they are all there. Various thymes surround the sundial, and box balls in clay pots stand on the semicircular brick paving.

It is a great tribute to Dick's energy and powers of organization that somehow he managed to have the whole garden laid out, labelled and ready for the show's May opening in Montreal. Since then, as promised, the gardens have been maintained by the staff of the Botanic Garden. It is thanks to them that the herb, bee and butterfly garden is kept in such good condition.

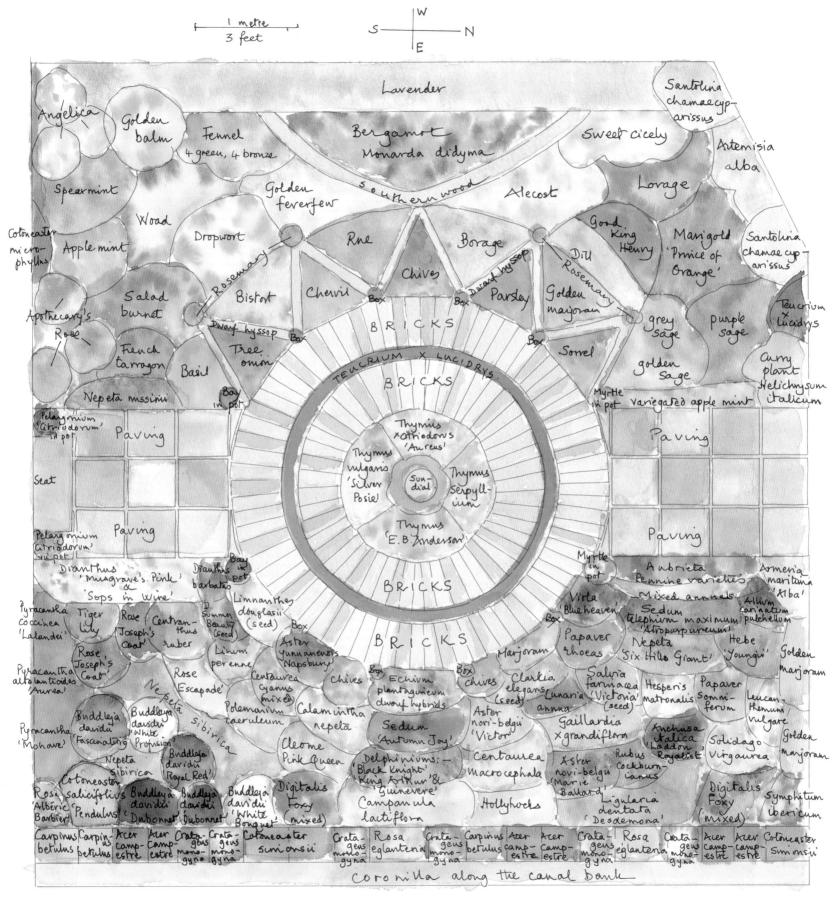

A SCENTED GARDEN

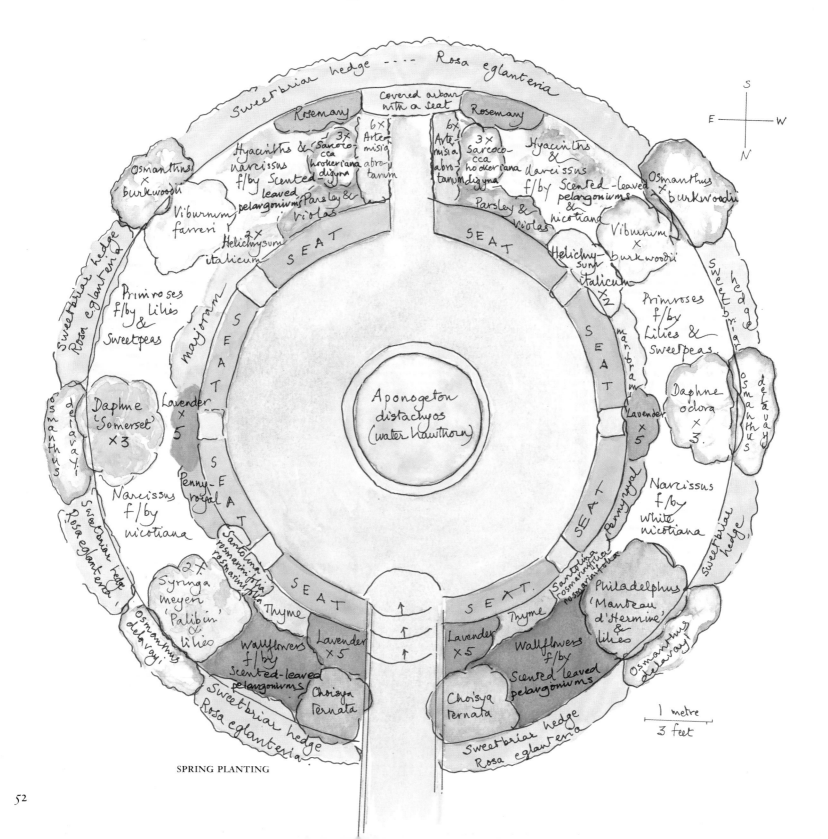

Sweetbriar hedge ---- Rosa eglanteria

Covered arbour with a seat

Rosemary

Rosemary

6× Artemisia abrotanum

6× Artemisia abrotanum

3× Sarcococca hookeriana digyna

3× Sarcococca hookeriana digyna

Hyacinths & narcissus f/by Scented leaved pelargoniums

Hyacinths & narcissus f/by Scented-leaved pelargoniums & nicotiana

Osmanthus × burkwoodii

Osmanthus × burkwoodii

Parsley & violas

Parsley & violas

Viburnum farreri

Viburnum × burkwoodii

Helichrysum italicum

Helichrysum italicum ×2

SEAT

SEAT

SEAT

SEAT

Sweetbriar hedge Rosa eglanteria

Sweetbriar hedge

Primroses f/by Lilies & sweetpeas

Primroses f/by Lilies & sweetpeas

Marjoram

marjoram

Osmanthus delavayi

Osmanthus delavayi

Daphne 'Somerset' ×3

Daphne odora ×3.

Lavender ×5

Lavender ×5

Aponogeton distachyos (water hawthorn)

Narcissus f/by nicotiana

Narcissus f/by white nicotiana

Penny-royal

Pennyroyal

SEAT

SEAT

Santolina rosmarinifolia rosmarinifolia

Santolina rosmarinifolia rosmarinifolia

Sweetbriar hedge Rosa eglanteria

Sweetbriar hedge

2× Syringa meyeri 'Palibin' & lilies

Philadelphus 'Manteau d'Hermine' & lilies

Thyme

Thyme

SEAT

SEAT.

Lavender ×5

Lavender ×5

Wallflowers f/by Scented-leaved pelargoniums

Wallflowers f/by Scented leaved pelargoniums

Osmanthus delavayi

Osmanthus delavayi

Choisya Ternata

Choisya Ternata

Sweetbriar hedge Rosa eglanteria

Sweetbriar hedge Rosa eglanteria

1 metre
3 feet

SPRING PLANTING

EVERY GARDEN DESIGN demands a different approach. Here at Luton Hoo in Bedfordshire, the late Nicholas Phillips asked me to help him create a scented garden, an invitation that I found especially appealing. Perfume is so volatile, and to reach its greatest potential it should be contained. Here I had the perfect situation.

The site is triangular. There are new office buildings on two sides and on the third is a line of trees, with another building only a short distance away. Many of the windows look down on the site, so the view must be enticing. What is most important, though, is that the garden should be a pleasant place where the people who work in the offices will enjoy walking and sitting.

We decided on a circular design enclosed by a hedge of sweetbriar (*Rosa eglanteria*) punctuated by six osmanthus. The small pink flowers of the rose are scented, but its special joy is the pervading apple fragrance of the leaves, which wafts to you all through summer and autumn, especially when the foliage is damp with dew or rain. The shining evergreen leaves of the osmanthus help to protect the garden from winter winds, and in spring its white, jasmine-like flowers have a strong honey scent that carries on the air.

There is only one entrance, through the hedge, with steps down into the inner circle, where a path is excavated out to a depth of 50cm (20in). I planned that the central feature should be a pool, filled with scented water hawthorn, *Aponogeton distachyos*. However, when the garden was laid out the pool was replaced by a stone sculpture which cleverly echoes the circular shape.

There are seats at the level of the surrounding beds, so that people who have time to sit in the garden can enjoy the scents of the low-growing plants. Immediately behind and beside the seats are thymes in variety, lavender, pennyroyal, the green santolina with an intense astringent

Above: Narcissus 'Charter' *is a beautiful large-cupped daffodil, pale yellow and sweetly scented. It flowers in mid-spring and is delightful as a companion to* Daphne odora 'Aureomarginata', *or growing around a later-flowering syringa or philadelphus. It is, however, only available from specialist bulb suppliers and may be hard to find. The old-fashioned pheasant's eye narcissus would make a good alternative choice.*

Right: Viburnum farreri – *an old favourite under its former name of* V. fragrans – *is the first of the fragrant viburnums to flower. The pale pink buds open to produce tight clusters of white flowers tinged with pink.*

scent, marjoram, parsley and the grey curry plant, *Helichrysum italicum*. The extra seat opposite the entrance has *Artemisia abrotanum* and rosemary nearby. Most of these have fragrant foliage that can be enjoyed right through the year. However, since sometimes leaves must be brushed against, squeezed or touched before they release their perfume, I have mixed in scented flowers. In spring the thymes are backed with wallflowers, the pennyroyal with narcissus, the marjoram with primroses, the parsley with hyacinths and narcissus.

The shrubs of medium height have been chosen to make a succession of bloom and fragrance. In winter and spring the first to scent the air will be *Viburnum farreri*, and this is followed by *V. × burkwoodii*. Both remain in flower for two or three months. The sarcococcas (sweet box) bear their small white flowers in late winter. In early spring *Daphne odora* 'Aureomarginata' follows on

The deliciously scented Madonna lily, Lilium candidum *(above), a favourite plant of cottage gardens, flowers crisp and white at midsummer. The flowers of the tobacco plant,* Nicotiana alata *(below), come in red and white and a wide range of colours in between. All have a heady fragrance.*

The deep pink buds of Daphne 'Somerset' (above) open to starry clusters of pale pink flowers during late spring and early summer.

from the viburnums. By late spring, and continuing into summer, the pale pink flowers of *Daphne* 'Somerset' are opening to waft their delicious scent upon the air. Also in early summer, the interesting *Syringa meyeri* 'Palibin' offers the surprisingly powerful scent of its dense panicles of pale purple flowers.

Philadelphus 'Manteau d'Hermine' is the star turn at midsummer. This compact philadelphus fits neatly into a small garden. At this season the lilies are growing through the shrubs, and the bulbs, primroses and wallflowers of spring have been replaced by tobacco plants – *Nicotiana sylvestris* and *N. alata* – sweet peas and scented-leaved pelargoniums. By autumn the nicotianas will have finished flowering and been removed, but the pelargoniums can be enjoyed until the first frosts. After that the leaves of the santolina, lavender, artemisia and helichrysum will provide perfume until the first flowers of *Viburnum farreri* open, and the year's cycle starts once again.

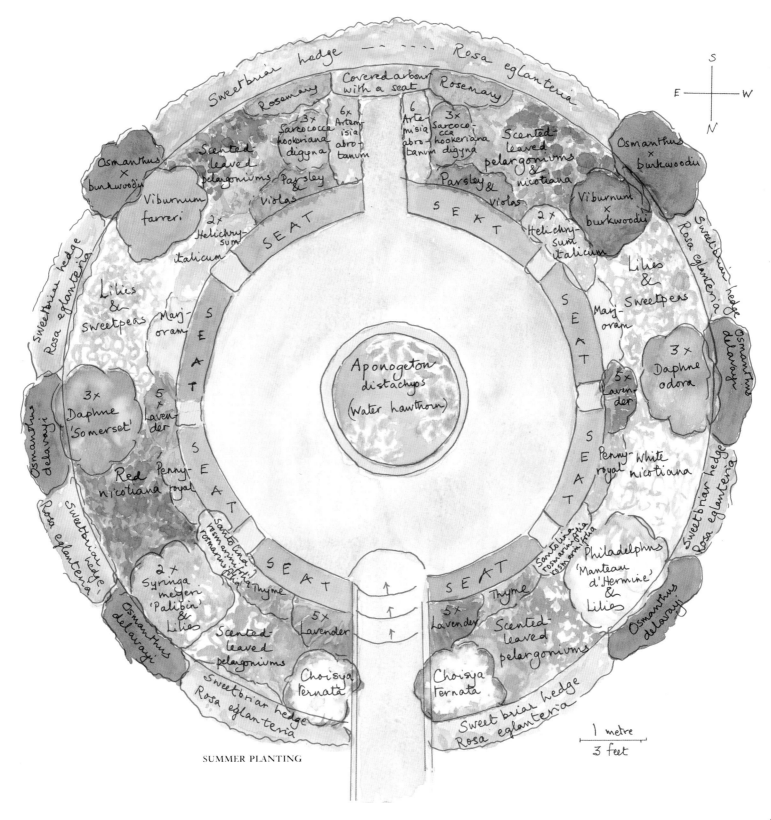

SUMMER PLANTING

A KNOT PATTERN FOR YEAR-ROUND INTEREST

*W*HEN A GARDEN *I know changes hands and the new owners invite me to give advice, I am often on the horns of a dilemma. This was the case with the Gloucestershire garden of Chapter Manor, where I had spent many Sunday afternoons playing tennis. Several years later the new owner, Lord Fanshawe, told me that he wanted to make an anniversary garden for his wife. How, I wondered, could I interfere with my old friend's garden? I went along, and there to my delight was a space, looked out on from the dining room and principal bedroom windows, which Lord Fanshawe suggested was an ideal site for a knot garden.*

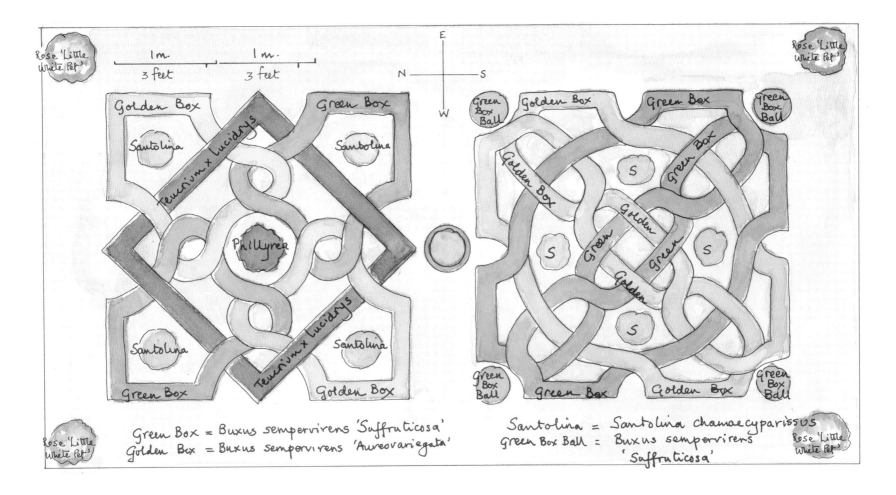

Rose 'Little White Pet'

1m. / 3 feet   1m. / 3 feet

Golden Box   Green Box

Santolina   Santolina

Teucrium x Lucidrys

Phillyrea

Santolina   Santolina

Teucrium x Lucidrys

Green Box   Golden Box

Rose 'Little White Pet'

Green Box = Buxus sempervirens 'Suffruticosa'
Golden Box = Buxus sempervirens 'Aureovariegata'

Rose 'Little White Pet'

Green Box Ball   Golden Box   Green Box   Green Box Ball

Golden Box

S

Green Box

Green

Golden

S   S

Green

Golden

S

Green Box Ball   Green Box   Golden Box   Green Box Ball

Rose 'Little White Pet'

Santolina = Santolina chamaecyparissus
Green Box Ball = Buxus sempervirens 'Suffruticosa'

E / N — S / W

The knot patterns are well defined when seen from above. The left-hand design is taken from Gervase Markham, the one on the right is Stephen Blake's 'True Lovers' Knot'. The corner detail is from the 'True Lovers' Knot'. The interlacing threads are clipped to give the illusion that they pass over and under each other.

The formality of a knot garden would make a complete contrast to the rest of the garden, where the river winds its way through lawns and shrubs and closely planted mixed borders. There was space for two 3m (10ft) square knots, symmetrically sited to be seen from the windows. This allowed for a gravel path 1m (39in) wide to surround them, and a path between.

There was a strong love of detail and design in sixteenth- and seventeenth-century Europe: knot-like patterns were used as decorative motifs in panelling, ceilings, book binding and floor tiles, as well as in embroidered dresses and robes. So it is not surprising that the knot motif should also have travelled outdoors, and appeared as living knots in gardens.

For Chapter Manor I tried several patterns, some of my own invention and

others from old books, but inevitably came back to the two patterns we had already used at Barnsley House. They are simple enough to fit into a comparatively small space. One is from Gervase Markham's 1616 *The Countrie Farm* (his translation of the French *La Maison Rustique*), and the other, the 'True Lovers' Knot', comes from Stephen Blake's book *The Compleat Gardener's Practice*, of 1664. Markham explains that you first make your design on paper and then add grid lines. Then, using cord and pegs, stretch out this grid on the ground, and copy the knot over them using dry sand.

Each interlacing thread of a knot should be made of a different evergreen. Here we used wall germander and two different varieties of box, which can all be clipped finely, to emphasize the 'overs and unders' of the threads.

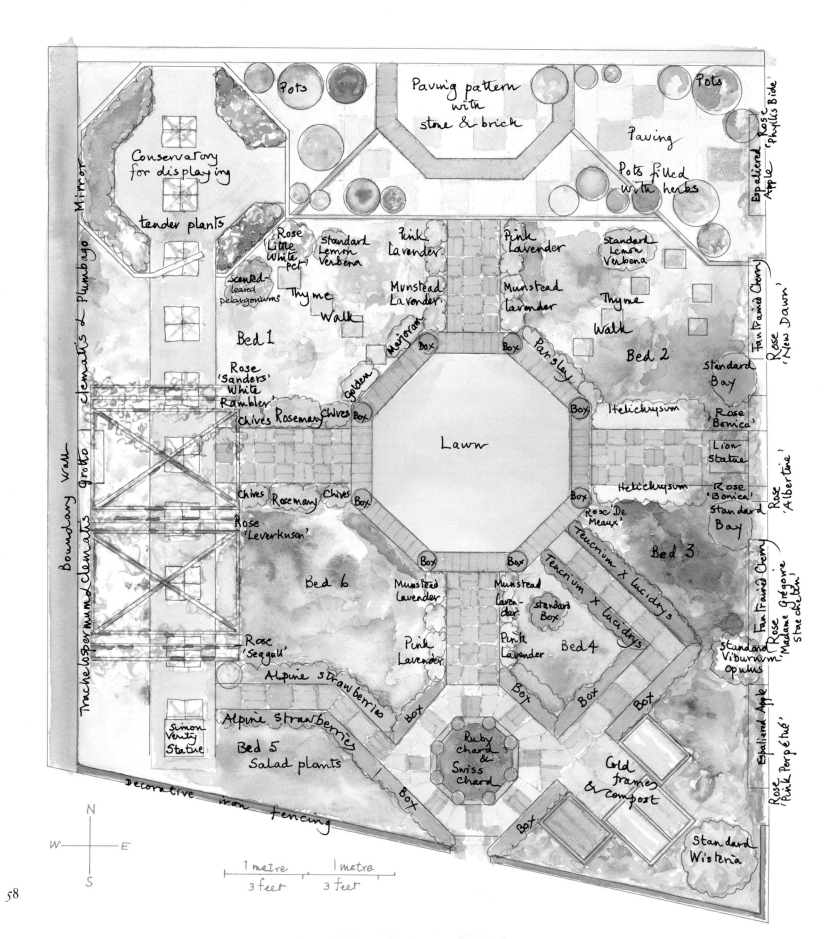

Pots

Paving pattern with stone & brick

Paving

Pots

Conservatory for displaying

tender plants

Pots filled with herbs

Espaliered Apple 'Phyllis Bide'

Rose 'Little White Pet'

Standard Lemon Verbena

Pink Lavender

Pink Lavender

Standard Lemon Verbena

Scented-leaved pelargoniums

Thyme Walk

Munstead Lavender

Munstead Lavender

Thyme Walk

Clematis & Plumbago

Mirror

Bed 1

Fan Trained Cherry

Rose 'New Dawn'

Marjoram

Box

Box

Parsley

Bed 2

Standard Bay

Rose 'Sanders' White Rambler'

Golden

Box

Helichrysum

Rose 'Bonica'

Grotto

Chives

Rosemary

Chives

Box

Lion Statue

Lawn

Boundary wall

Chives

Rosemary

Chives

Box

Box

Helichrysum

Rose 'Bonica'

Rose 'Albertine'

Rose 'De Meaux'

Standard Bay

Rose 'Leverkusen'

Box

Box

Teucrium x lucidrys

Bed 3

Trachelospermum and clematis

Bed 6

Munstead Lavender

Munstead Lavender

Teucrium x lucidrys

Fan Trained Cherry

Rose 'Madame Grégoire Staechelin'

standard Box

Rose 'Seagull'

Pink Lavender

Pink Lavender

Bed 4

Standard Viburnum opulus

Alpine strawberries

Box

Box

Box

Espaliered Apple

Simon Verity Statue

Alpine strawberries

Box

Cold frames & compost

Rose 'Pink Perpétue'

Bed 5
Salad plants

Ruby chard & Swiss chard

Box

decorative iron fencing

Box

Standard Wisteria

N

W   E

S

58

1 metre   1 metre
3 feet   3 feet

A SMALL TOWN GARDEN

W HEN I DESIGNED *a small town garden for the Chelsea Flower Show of 1992 I had the conditions of a real town garden very much in mind. I hoped that visitors would look around and feel inspired by some of the ideas we included – that they might say to each other 'We can do this at home', or 'This is a great idea for our garden.'*

The open gate in the decorative blue iron railings invites you into the garden. Walk along the path to the pergola and the conservatory beyond.

I was delighted to be invited by the London *Evening Standard* to design a garden for Chelsea 1992. I felt excited – while I had walked round the show each May I had often secretly thought what fun it would be to make a Chelsea garden. Now I had the opportunity.

This was August 1991, and I imagined that as soon as the location, shape and dimensions of the site were defined, I would have all the winter slowly to dream up the theme and plan. My complacency was soon shattered by a request from the show committee to submit by mid-September a drawing to include the hard landscaping and detailed planting. So my dreaming days were numbered. I had to get down to some hard thinking. An early practical thought was to involve my friend and colleague John Hill, of Sherborne Gardens in Gloucestershire. John agreed to undertake all the hard landscaping – in the event he did far more than this, and was a tremendous help throughout.

As the garden was sponsored by a London newspaper, naturally it would be a town garden. In my thoughts the owners of this house and garden would be busy people, keen gardeners who would cherish this small area as a place to relax and work in at weekends and in the evenings. They would enjoy the very tasks of gardening,

59

as well as the consequent pleasures of germinating seeds, growing a few vegetables, herbs and other scented plants, and having flowers to pick. Their time would be limited, so the planting must be realistic and practical. But I thought that they would like having a tiny conservatory to nurture a few special tender plants through the winter.

The site we were allocated was approximately 10 x 8m (33 x 28ft) and had gangways on three sides. This was a great advantage, as three open sides meant three different aspects, and we made the most of this – but we had to remember that in reality a typical town garden would probably be enclosed on three or even four sides.

On the south boundary we put some beautiful old railings, painted a distinctive blue, which were supplied by Hughie Powell of the decorative metalwork firm HMP. We felt we should give the east (west-facing) boundary the illusion of being an enclosing wall. What we actually did was to erect a series of arches for climbers all along this side. The visitors to the show would have a different view into the garden through each arch. The climber-clad arches could be used as an effective partial screen in a town or country garden, or the same climbers could be grown against a wall.

On the north side we created an interior *trompe l'œil* effect: the visitors walking along this gangway should have the feeling that they were inside the house looking through two windows and a door into the garden. Changes of level are always important, especially in small gardens, so beside the 'wall' we constructed a raised paved area.

The fourth side, facing east, was the dividing wall between our garden and our neighbour's, and by regulation had to be 1.8m (6ft) high. Here on this wall was the ideal place for the grotto I had asked Diana Reynell to design. Here too we could place a pergola to support more climbing plants.

Whatever the size of your garden, it is vitally important to have satisfying views from your bedroom, kitchen or study windows. These scenes are like stage sets, with tracery and shapes in winter, embellished each spring and summer with leaves and flowers.

Walking round the garden is a different sensation, one you can take slowly or at a hurried pace – as you progress along your borders, you can turn round and see them from a different viewpoint. The late Russell Page, that doyen of twentieth-century garden designers, explained to me that as you walk from your house the garden must invite you on; you should not feel there is a clutter of plants impeding your progress. Every garden needs an open space for you to walk into, a place where you can take a deep breath, contemplate your surroundings and enjoy the moment.

So, true to Russell's teaching, I designed a small octagonal lawn, with box balls and brick edging emphasizing the shape, enclosed by beds divided by paths. Once I had the ground plan measurements it was not too difficult to work out. Initially we pegged out the boundary shape on my own lawn, adding the paths, borders and pergola. Doing it this way, we could be confident that the proportions were correct and the vistas worked.

As soon as the site was ours on 30th April the hard landscaping began. The ground was stripped, the paving and the brick paths were laid, the pergola and arches and the conservatory were erected. All this took four of John Hill's men ten days.

Then we could start planting in the six main beds. All the plants had been grown on in containers, ready to be dropped in with their pots hidden by imported compost.

The two beds nearest the house (beds 1 and 2) were kept to herbs and scented plants. They were outlined with lavender, marjoram, rosemary, chives, parsley and the curry plant, and had a stepping stone and thyme path through them to make herb picking easier. The other herbs I used were basil, fennel, lovage, chamomile, golden mint, purple and grey sage, infilled with 'Tom Thumb' and red lettuce, rocket and corn salad. The standard lemon verbenas

The arches along the east boundary of the Chelsea garden.

THE PLANTING IN THE MAIN BEDS

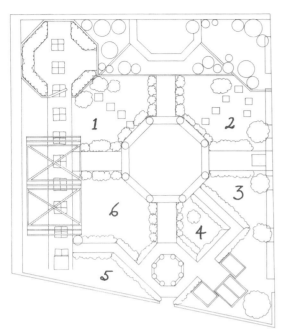

BED 1
Rose 'Sanders' White Rambler'
Rose 'Little White Pet'
Box
Lemon verbena
Sage
Lavender
Rosemary
Lovage
Thyme in variety
Chamomile in variety
Salad rocket
Golden marjoram
True Greek oregano
Basil
Golden eau-de-cologne mint
Chives
'Tom Thumb' lettuce
Red lettuce
Corn salad

BED 2
Rose 'Bonica'
Lemon verbena
Purple sage
Bronze fennel
Lavender
Sorrel
Parsley
Thyme in variety
Chamomile in variety
Basil
Winter savory
Helichrysum italicum curry plant
Saxifraga × urbium London pride
'Tom Thumb' lettuce

BED 3
Rose 'Bonica'
Rose 'De Meaux'
Viburnum opulus
Convolvulus cneorum
Delphiniums
Lavender
Hesperis matronalis dame's violets
Thalictrum aquilegiifolium
Schizanthus
Aquilegias
Hostas
Polemonium caeruleum Jacob's ladder
Agrostemma githago 'Milas' corn cockle
Alliums
Pansies
Scabious
Helichrysum italicum curry plant
Saxifraga × urbium London pride
Teucrium × lucidrys wall germander

BED 4
Bay
Box
Lavender
cabbage
lettuce
Teucrium × lucidrys wall germander

BED 5
Box
Carrots
Chicory
Lettuce
Alpine strawberries

BED 6
Rose 'Leverkusen'
Rose 'Seagull'
Box
Delphiniums
Irises
Hesperis matronalis dame's violets
Osteospermum
Sedum
Oxalis adenophylla
Hostas
Artemisia ludoviciana
Heuchera 'Palace Purple'
Alliums
Polemonium caeruleum Jacob's ladder
Cornflowers
Geranium 'Ballerina'
Lavender
Rosemary
Schizanthus
Scabious
Cabbage
Golden French beans
Alpine strawberries

In a planting near the shell grotto, the yellow in the bold, sword-like leaves of Acorus calamus *'Variegatus' echoed the yellow flowers of* Euphorbia polychroma *and provided a foil for purple aquilegias and pansies.*

On pages 62-3: *A view across the garden shows the decorative shell and stone grotto constructed by Diana Reynell. Cleverly devised to fit in a small space, the pergola supported climbing roses (from left to right),* Rosa 'Seagull', R. 'Leverkusen' *and* R. 'Sanders' White Rambler', *their pale colours well set off by the apricot-coloured wall. In front, eight clipped box balls in weathered clay pots defined the corners of the lawn. The planting in the beds was a mixture of herbs, salad crops, scented plants and flowers and foliage to pick, while the small conservatory provided the opportunity to overwinter tender plants.*

Left: *The basic rhythm of the garden was set by the octagonal central lawn with its brick edging and box balls.*

Above, right: *In bed 3 we kept to pink and blue with some blue-reds and white, using* Rosa 'Bonica' *and* R. 'De Meaux', *and a mixture of infillers that included alliums, aquilegias,* Thalictrum aquilegiifolium, *dame's violets and schizanthus. In the pot on the left is a standard bay, with a twisted stem.*

Below, right: *Bed 1 was devoted to herbs and salad plants. In the small area shown here we had golden marjoram, thymes, red lettuce and basil as well as a standard box ball.*

Below, far right: *Pots on the terrace held Rupert Golby's decorative planting. Fennel mixed well with golden grass and variegated honeysuckle; a clump of chives was encircled by golden thyme; different thymes made patterns around a miniature standard box ball; a saxifrage had made a solid cushion in a shallow pan; and* Viola labradorica *surrounded bronze fennel and Bowles' golden grass.*

were the star turns.

There were more herbs on the nearby terrace, this time in the form of miniature herb gardens planted by my colleague Rupert Golby in various clay pots and containers. These 'herbscapes' were beautiful then and looked exciting for months afterwards.

The next small bed on the east side (bed 3) was lined with rose 'De Meaux', *Helichrysum italicum* and *Teucrium × lucidrys*. The colour theme here was pink and blue, with schizanthus, aquilegias, delphiniums, corn cockles, *Thalictrum aquilegiifolium*, scabious, Jacob's ladder, pansies, and the round heads of *Allium karataviense* and *A. aflatunense*. Rose 'Bonica' was used both here and in bed 2. Its long flowering season makes it especially valuable.

The public would see all the beds on this side through the arches, unlike the owners, whose view would be from the lawn with the arches and imaginary wall as a backdrop. When planting I had to keep this in mind. The climbing roses for the arches were 'Phyllis Bide', 'New Dawn', 'Albertine', 'Madame Grégoire Staechelin' and 'Pink Perpétué', their colours harmonizing with the planting behind them. To reinforce the illusion of the wall, we had fan-trained cherries and espaliered apples growing inside the arches, placed as they

Above: *Simon Verity's pensive stone lady, with her necklace and cornucopia of flowers, became a focus of attention, standing at the end of the pergola. The patterned tiles set between the terracotta slabs came from Portugal.*

Left: *In bed 6, mauve, blue, pink and a splash of grey combined to create a cottage garden effect. The leaves of cabbage,* Sedum *'Autumn Joy',* Hosta *'Zounds',* Heuchera *'Palace Purple' and the sword-like foliage of* Iris *'Loretii' blended and contrasted in colour and shape. The round heads of* Allium aflatunense *pushed through delphiniums, dame's violets and Jacob's ladder, while grey* Artemisia ludoviciana *and scabious 'Clive Greaves' grew together in good companionship.*

would be if growing naturally against the wall. I have to confess, though, that we moved away from the illusion with a magnificent statue of a lioness, copied faithfully from the Animal Wall at Cardiff Castle and lent to us by the garden statue suppliers Recollections. We placed it under the centre arch, looking out on the passers-by!

On the west side, bed 6, adjoining the pergola, was filled with foliage plants, *Oxalis adenophylla*, hostas and cabbage, with flower colour added by dame's violets, schizanthus and osteospermum. The edging here was of lavender, rosemary and chives, box and alpine strawberries, and there was still space for a row of golden-podded French beans. The adjacent beds, 4 and 5, had salad plants – a line of early carrots grown in troughs, chicory and a variety of lettuces.

I was planting from 14th May until the moment the judges were due to arrive on the 18th, helped one day by my gardeners Andy and Les. During that time the railings were being put up along the south boundary. Here I had hoped to have gourds climbing, but they are an autumn show and were not mature enough by May, so instead we used a selection of scented-leaved pelargoniums.

Now we have travelled almost all around, except for the west side story. Here was the decorative metal pergola, giving support for three pairs of climbing roses, 'Leverkusen', 'Sanders' White Rambler' and 'Seagull', and shade for ferns and hostas; providing, too, a wonderful frame for my much-loved lady gardener statue with her cornucopia of flowers, carved by the sculptor Simon Verity and given to my husband David for his seventieth birthday. It was her first and only visit to London, where she was admired and extolled, and I hope she does not now find life at Barnsley less exciting. Here also was the elegant conservatory made by Derek Elliott and, on the wall, Diana Reynell's sparkling grotto.

The Cardiff lioness, framed by London pride and Rosa *'Bonica', kept guard over our garden.*

During the few heady, unseasonably hot days of Chelsea week, we forgot the anxiety, the hard work, the unaccountably long hours involved during ten months of preparation. For me, perhaps, the drama of the destruction of my garden (along with all the others) will remain memorable, even as the details of the planting fade. But the plan and photographs stand as a reminder. Best of all are the appreciative remarks made to me during Chelsea, and touching letters written afterwards. So many people have said that they knew it was a Rosemary Verey garden because it reminded them of my planting at Barnsley – a compliment, I hope! The Barnsley garden will go on, while Chelsea was a garden of a week. It was great fun while it lasted.

SUMMER BORDERS

*L*ONGLEAT HOUSE *in Wiltshire is famous for its magnificent trees and parkland, and for the work carried out there by the great garden designer Russell Page (as well as for lions, of course). So I was especially pleased to be invited by the late Marquess and the Marchioness of Bath to make a new planting plan for two long herbaceous borders.*

Below: *The front corners of both borders are densely planted: round heads of* Allium karataviense *appear through the young leaves of* Sedum *'Autumn Joy'.*

Right: *At the back corners of the hot border, bold clumps of* Polygonum amplexicaule *'Atrosanguineum' flower throughout the summer, providing a strong statement.*

YEW HEDGE

Border with 'hot' colours

Yew arbour facing ↑

Border with 'cool' colours

1m / 3ft 1m / 3ft

Grass

Tennis court

E · S · N · W

Below, left: *The flat-domed heads of Scabiosa* caucasica *'Clive Greaves' consist of many small flowers surrounded by bracts of a deeper lavender-blue, excellent for cutting. The seedheads that follow are also decorative.*

Below, right: *The peach-leaved bellflower,* Campanula persicifolia, *will produce a succession of new buds so long as dying flowers are removed. If this plant is allowed to self-seed there will be more blue than white volunteers.*

The two borders run the length and more of the hard tennis court opposite, and are separated from it by a grass lawn 3m (10ft) wide. Backed by a high yew hedge, they are divided by the convex side of a yew arbour that forms part of the hedge. Between hedge and borders there is a narrow grass path. This makes for easy access, needed for clipping the yew and working on the back of the beds.

In replanting the borders we were to concentrate on the summer months, the peak time for visitors to Longleat, and in high summer 1985 I spent an afternoon with the Marchioness of Bath, discussing with her which plants she liked and the basic colour schemes she hoped to have. A skilled gardener herself, she quickly conveyed her ideas to me.

At that time the borders were identical, but it did not take long to decide that they should have different plans. One bed would have 'cool' blues and mauves, blue-reds and pinks with white. The other would have 'hot' yellows, orange, mahogany-red and bright red.

It is much easier to plan and plant up a border from scratch than to juggle new plants between existing ones, which is what we tried to do here. We went through the borders in detail, deciding which clumps should be discarded and which should change beds. This required considerable thought, as the existing planting was very

Above: *The cinnabar-red* Crocosmia *'Lucifer' makes an eye-catching display throughout the summer. At Longleat we divided existing clumps and used the plants to provide a bright feature, surrounded by yellows, at the centre of the hot border.*

Right: *The leaves of a good specimen of* Melissa officinalis *'Aurea' glow at the front of the hot border. If the flowering stems are removed, new, well-coloured growth will take over. Seedlings are green.*

Bed 2

Polygonum amplexicaule 'Atrosanguineum' · Heliopsis 'Summer Sun' · Yellow Hollyhocks · Thalictrum aquilegifolium · Helianthus · Ligularia dentata · Polygonum amplexicaule 'Atrosanguineum'

Achillea filipendulina 'Gold Plate' · Ligularia 'The Rocker' · Gaillardia 'Croftway Yellow' · Crocosmia 'Lucifer' · Crocosmia 'Lucifer' · Gaillardia 'Mandarin' · Coreopsis · Monarda 'Cambridge Scarlet'

Sedum & Alliums · Hemerocallis 'Golden Chimes' · Spiraea japonica 'Gold Flame' · Potentilla 'Yellow Queen' · Spiraea japonica 'Gold Flame' · Sedum & Alliums

Filipendula ulmaria 'Aurea' · Golden marjoram · Achillea 'Moonshine' · Golden marjoram · Helichrysum 'Sulphur Light' · Melissa officinalis 'Aurea'

mixed and I could detect no planned purpose to it.

Lady Bath did not like the tellima or the gypsophila, finding them too ephemeral, with insufficient impact. The macleya was too gloomy (I do agree with her). The white daisies, *Chrysanthemum magnificum* and *C. maximum,* were too coarse, and the *Artemisia* 'Silver Queen' became untidy. The Japanese anemones, planted between the *Agapanthus* Headbourne hybrids, flowered too late. These plants were all to go.

In the end, there was comparatively little that we wanted to keep. The heuchera, the scabious and the blue monarda, the hardy geraniums and the agapanthus would all go to the blue and pink bed 1, and the hemerocallis to the red-yellow bed 2. *Crocosmia* 'Lucifer', which was in both beds, was to go in bed 2, massed in two adjacent groups. *Sedum* 'Autumn Joy' had been divided and replanted in too many places: it should be concentrated on the corners of both beds and in the centre front of bed 1. The sedums should still have *Allium karataviense* and *A. christophii* planted among them.

Some ingredients of the hot border. Ligularia dentata (above, left) is a valuable perennial for bold planting in deep, rich soil. The undersides of the leaves and the stems are dark purple. Every part of Monarda didyma *'Cambridge Scarlet' (above, centre) is aromatic. Coreopsis lanceolata (above, right) is in bloom for weeks in summer. Helianthus 'Capenoch Sun' (below) is a reliable, long-lasting cut flower.*

Right: *The magnificent* Romneya coulteri *is a native of southern California. The crinkled petals – here, suffused with evening light – surround a globe of yellow stamens.*

Below: *Blues for late summer and autumn interest:* Agapanthus *Headbourne hybrids growing with* Acanthus spinosus *in the cool border. In the foreground are the striking seedheads of* Eryngium giganteum, *Miss Willmott's ghost, and* Salvia nemorosa *'East Friesland'. It is wise to stake the heavy acanthus heads individually: then they will look dramatic until they are cut down in late autumn.*

I suggested to the head gardener that a work programme should be drawn up. Provided he could muster a sufficient workforce, it would be much easier if the two beds were worked simultaneously. Each clump should be labelled, dug up and moved to a position beside the border it was meant for, or removed elsewhere. When cleared, the borders must be well dug and manured, and the soil left to settle for a few days.

I delivered the first consignment of new plants in mid-autumn. When I had placed these in their positions I was able to assess the gaps and work out what was needed to fill the beds so that they would look generously planted by next summer. It turned out that we needed about ninety more plants and these were brought over a couple of weeks later.

This border is now (in 1993) seven years old, and changes have certainly been made over the years, but the main theme remains the same: one border with blues, pinks and blue-reds, the other with brighter tones of yellow through to hot reds. Borders are forever changing and developing, but I hope that the present Marquess will one day call me back to consolidate my colour thoughts in these borders.

Left: *The reliable* Campanula lactiflora *produces panicles of flowers throughout the summer.*

Above: *Tall flower spikes of* Cimicifuga racemosa *make a fine display in late summer and early autumn.*

Bed 1

73

Apple Tunnel   Pear tunnel   Malus 'Golden Hornet'

A WALLED GARDEN

T HE WALLED GARDEN *at*
Ascott Place, in Berkshire,
dates back to the nineteenth
century, when labour was both
plentiful and cheap, and the
head gardener was expected to
produce fresh vegetables daily
for the household. The large
range of glasshouses had once
provided the opportunity to grow
exotic pot plants for the house,
thousands of seedlings for the
carpet bedding, orchids, apricots
and peaches.

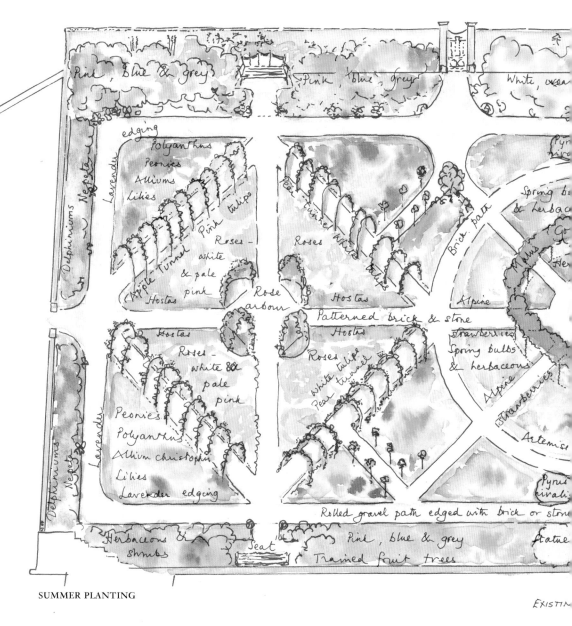

Pink, blue & grey   Pink, blue, grey   White, cream

edging
Polyanthus
Peonies
Alliums
Lilies

Lavender
Nepeta
Delphiniums

Pink tulips
Apple Tunnel White
Roses — white & pale pink
Hostas
Rose arbour

Roses
Pea tunnel White
Hostas

Brick path
Alpine
Patterned brick & stone
Hostas
strawberries
Spring bulbs & herbaceous
Alpine
Artemisia

Spring bulbs & herbaceous
Malus Golden Hornet

Hostas
Roses — white & pale pink
Peonies
Polyanthus
Allium christophii
Lilies
Lavender edging

Roses
White tulips
Pea tunnel

Strawberries
Pyrus salicifolia

Rolled gravel path edged with brick or stone

Herbaceous & shrubs   Seat   Pink, blue & grey   Statue
Trained fruit trees

SUMMER PLANTING

EXISTING

Trained fruit Trees

Herbaceous & shrubs   STATUE

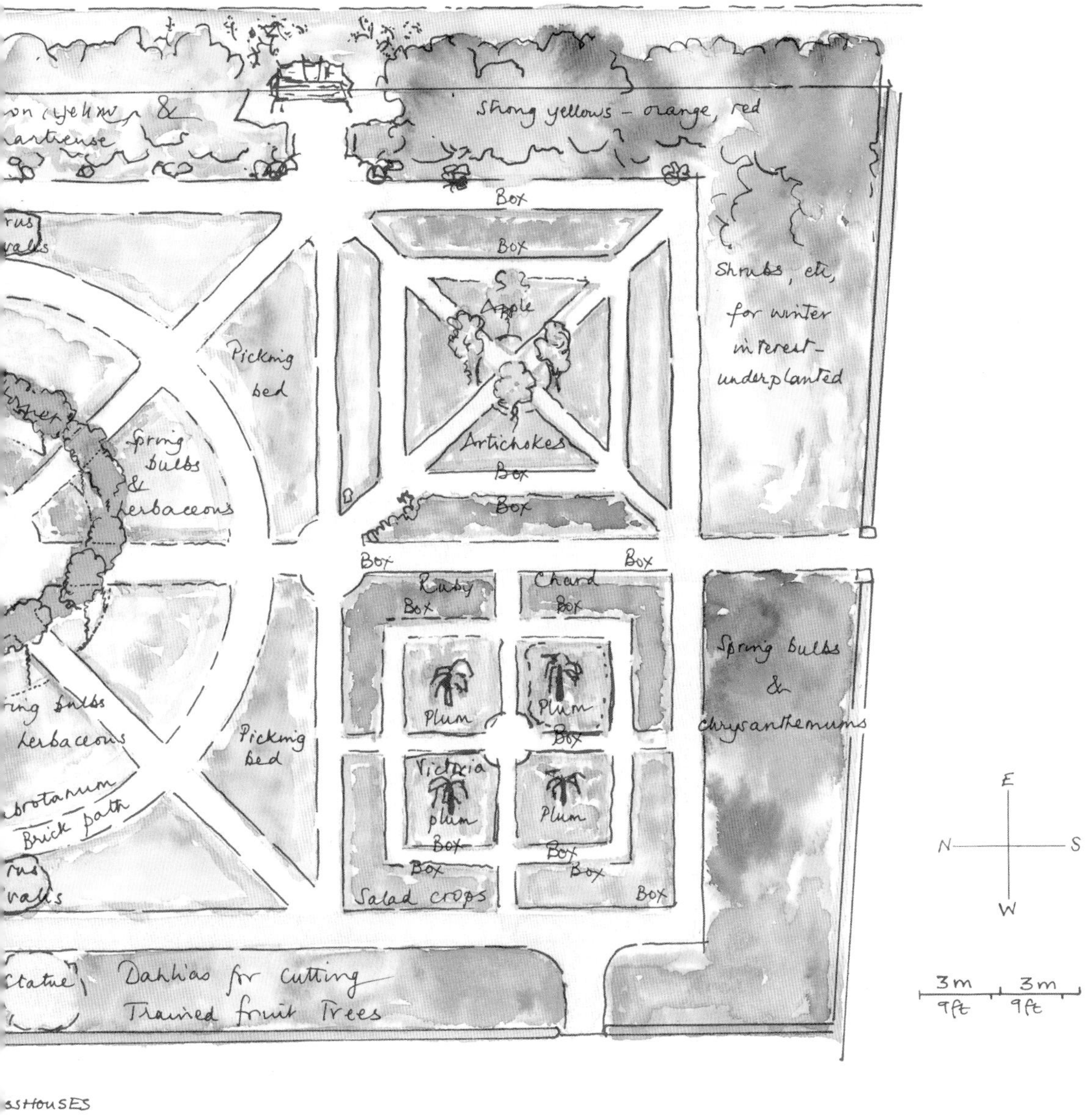

Strong yellows – orange, red
Box
Box
Apple
Shrubs, etc, for winter interest – underplanted
Picking bed
Spring bulbs & herbaceous
Artichokes
Box
Box
Box
Box
Ruby
Box
Chard
Box
Plum
Plum
Box
Victoria plum
Box
Plum
Box
Box
Salad crops
Box
Spring bulbs & Chrysanthemums
Picking bed
Brick path
Statue
Dahlias for cutting
Trained fruit Trees
E
N
S
W
3m
3m
9ft
9ft

These were the reflections that passed through my mind as I first walked in the walled garden on an autumn day in 1989. But the scene around me was very different from the one in my thoughts. A hard tennis court occupied one corner, and a derelict metal aviary was the central feature. Rough grass and weeds grew where there had been vegetables. The fruit trees once trained on the walls had been left unpruned, but they were not beyond recall.

I was there at the invitation of the family who had recently acquired the estate. My brief, at this point, was to give verbal suggestions for making the best of this walled garden. We decided that it should become a special, almost secret garden where the family and their guests would enjoy walking at all times of the year. The erstwhile Victorian vegetable garden would become a twentieth-century ornamental potager. To achieve this, both the tennis court and the aviary would have to go. As we walked round I tried to describe how there could be rose tunnels, patterned paths, scented shrubs and flowers for picking all though the year, as well as fruit and vegetables. A few days later I was given the go-ahead to prepare plans.

The garden inside the wall was 72 x 36m (80 x 40 yards), the long sides facing east

Trained fruit trees
STATUE
Dahlias for cutting

SPRING PLANTING

The blossom of Malus *'Golden Hornet'. Decorative and versatile, crab apples can be trained in an espalier against a wall, or to make a graceful open screen.*

and west. I had to work with the existing features, which included the wonderful high red brick walls, gates on all four sides and a 1.2m (4ft) path which ran around the perimeter of the garden, leaving a border 3m (10ft) wide along each wall. There was also a central path running from north to south. I chose to keep all these paths, as they must have been there for years, and would be necessary for working the garden.

The gate on the east side was the starting point for my design, as this would be the main entrance from the surrounding parkland, and it would frame the vista. Strong vistas are of the utmost importance in a formal garden, and my plan was going to be formal, with informal planting.

Basically, I planned to divide the garden into three parts, each with a different theme. For the section at the south end I designed two squares with narrow paths and beds to hold vegetables such as artichokes, salad crops and ruby chard. One of the squares was to be divided into four triangles, all planted with artichokes. These four beds could also contain dessert apples trained into goblet shapes. It is important to keep in mind the vertical effect. The apple trees, well trained and kept to around 2.5m (8ft) high, would provide height, and they would also offer both spring blossom and a handsome fruit crop after the artichokes had provided their harvest. The four narrow perimeter beds could hold more artichokes or have asparagus or strawberries, according to the wishes of the family.

The other square was to contain four square beds with embracing L-shaped borders. Each bed would hold a Victoria plum on a dwarfing stock. The variety I chose is appropriately called 'Pixy', and has branches that festoon downwards. This would be the place for salad crops. Lettuces would include the early 'Tom Thumb', the decorative 'Lollo Rosso', whose ruffled crinkly leaves are an intense crimson tapering down to pale green hearts, and the dramatic chicories (also known by their

Above: *The late-flowering tulip 'Angélique', with pink and white peony-like flowers, would make a delightful underplanting for apple trees in blossom.* Right: *Rose 'New Dawn', with blush-pink flowers, fruity fragrance and glossy leaves – a joy in any garden.*

Paeonia humilis *var.* villosa *has splendid foliage and flowers which, though short-lived, are sensationally beautiful.*

Rose 'Madame Isaac Pereire' produces its madder-crimson, richly scented flowers in bursts throughout the summer and autumn.

Rose 'Ispahan', one of the finest Damask roses, has double pink flowers and a delicious scent. It flowers profusely around midsummer.

Malus 'Golden Hornet'

Herbs & violas

Fountain

AUTUMN PLANTING

The dessert plum 'Victoria', grafted on a Pixy stock, is admirable for festooning.

Malus 'Golden Hornet' produces a wealth of golden crab apples in autumn.

Italian name of *radicchio*), 'Red Verona' and 'Red Treviso'. This last is the most beautiful of all, shaped like a small cos lettuce with slender deep burgundy leaves with bright white veins. Among the lettuces would be planted giant red mustard and salad rocket, also known as *arugula* and *roquette*.

The middle area was centred on the doorway through the west wall which leads into the glasshouse. The design for this section was based on concentric circles, with eight paths radiating from a fountain in the middle. Around the fountain there was to be a circle of *Malus* 'Golden Hornet', an idea inspired by Lady Salisbury, who used a crab apple circle in a garden she designed. The beds around the crab apples would have a mixture of spring bulbs and herbaceous plants, and I decided to edge them with alpine strawberries and southernwood.

For the area at the north end I planned apple and pear tunnels to form a square, with a central rose arbour. The roses here were to be white, pink and crimson. The pears were to be underplanted with white tulips and the apples with pink tulips, both carefully chosen to bloom at the same time as the trees were in blossom. The four central triangles created by the pattern of tunnels and paths would be filled with old-fashioned scented roses, and the outer triangles were to have polyanthus for spring, followed by peonies, alliums and masses of lilies, with an edging of lavender. There would be scent right through from spring to autumn.

I planned that the borders running all around the garden should have a colour theme. The soft greys, pinks, blues and mauves would be in the borders towards the north end. Here would be flowering shrubs for scent and winter structure, and delphiniums and peonies for picking. A strip of white, cream and pale yellow would act as a division between the cool colours and the strong reds, yellows and orange at the south end. A separate bed would have dahlias, grown for picking for the house. For the beds under the short south wall I chose a variety of winter-flowering shrubs – wintersweet, winter honeysuckle, witch hazels and viburnums – to be underplanted with spring bulbs followed by chrysanthemums.

The placing of the seats was important, as I wished this garden to be a restful place. If you look on the plan you will notice that from each of the seats there would be a view across the garden. There were to be scented plants on either side. The rose arbour would also have single seats in each quarter, and the fountain would have a low wall around it, just the right height to sit on.

Sadly, after I had dreamed up this 'paradise' garden, the estate was sold. My plans are still only in the mind, in rough outline. It would be such a delight to carry out the detailed planting.

Above right: *A tunnel of pears or apples is enchanting in blossom, pleasantly shady throughout the summer, and both handsome and useful when the trees fruit. Tunnels can be underplanted with hellebores and primulas, narcissus and tulips for spring, followed by annuals such as rudbeckia or nasturtiums for summer.*

Chrysanthemum *'Gold Margaret'* (right) *and* C. *'Salmon Margaret'* (far right). *Under the north-facing wall at Ascott Place, I planned to have a permanent planting of shrubs with winter interest, underplanted with spring bulbs followed by chrysanthemums. The chrysanthemums, grown for picking for the house, should be carefully chosen to co-ordinate with the colours of walls and curtains.*

Green box = Buxus sempervirens 'Suffruticosa'

Golden box = Buxus sempervirens 'Aureovariegata'

A COURTYARD KNOT GARDEN

I WAS DELIGHTED WHEN the Misses Barrie, owners of Orchard Farm House, in Broadway, Gloucestershire, invited me to suggest ideas to improve their courtyard. Orchard Farm House dates from the seventeenth century, though it was altered and enlarged later. The courtyard, enclosed on three sides by the house and overlooked by many windows, is the perfect site for a knot garden.

Looking south-west, in summertime. The knot garden can be seen from three sides of the house.

This was 1985, and I had not then gone metric, so all my measurements were in feet and inches. The metric measurements given here in brackets are the precise equivalent of my imperial measurements, and could be followed to give patterns of exactly the same size. However, if you wished to draw up a design using metric measurements, it would be sensible to start from a more manageable basic unit.

The courtyard measures 28 x 33 ft (8.54 x 10.05m), so there was plenty of space to lay a York stone path, 10ft (3.05m) wide, down the centre. This enabled me to design two 8ft (2.44m) square knots, to be placed on each side of the path. They are simple knots adapted from patterns in Gervase Markham's book *The Countrie Farm*, of 1616. With their continuous interlacing threads made of box and wall germander they are intended to be infilled with gravel of different colours. The whole design makes a picture in itself, and an infill of gaudy flowers would spoil it.

There was also enough space to include some extra patterns in box. I hope these shapes both enhance the overall picture, and also invite closer inspection on their own account.

To lay it all out I first drew grid lines at 1in (2.5cm) intervals over my design, and diagonal lines from corner to corner on knots 3 and 4. I was using a scale of 1 to 24, as it suited me to have each inch on my paper representing 2ft on the ground. When I came to transfer the patterns to the ground I took with me plenty of bamboo canes, twine, dry sand and an improvised compass made of two sticks joined by a 2ft (60cm) length of twine. I also took a right-angle template, made with 1½in (4cm)

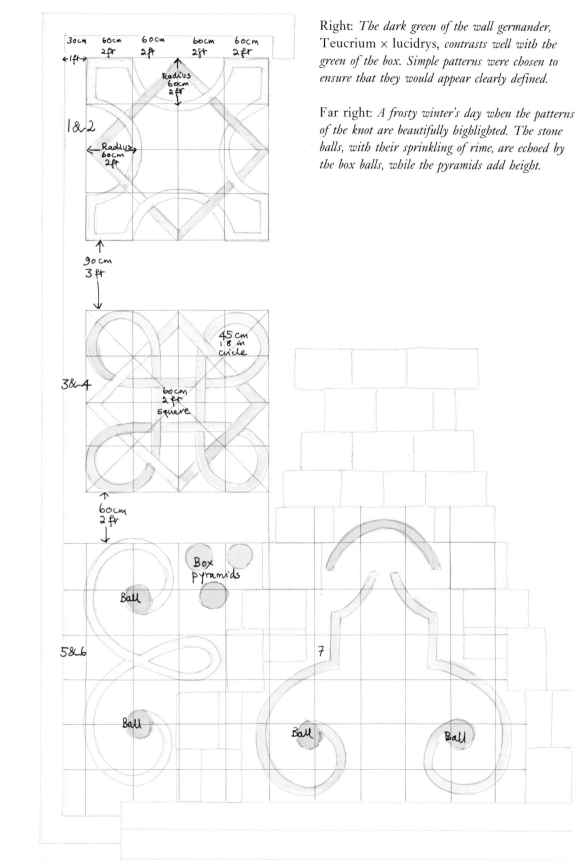

30cm 60cm 60cm 60cm 60cm
1ft 2ft 2ft 2ft 2ft

Radius
60cm
2ft

1&2

Radius
60cm
2ft

90cm
3ft

45cm
1.8 m
circle

3&4

60cm
2ft
square

60cm
2ft

Box
pyramids

Ball

5&6

Ball

7

Ball

Ball

Right: *The dark green of the wall germander,* Teucrium × lucidrys, *contrasts well with the green of the box. Simple patterns were chosen to ensure that they would appear clearly defined.*

Far right: *A frosty winter's day when the patterns of the knot are beautifully highlighted. The stone balls, with their sprinkling of rime, are echoed by the box balls, while the pyramids add height.*

pieces of wood, to help ensure that the corners were accurate at 90°.

My first job was to mark out the grid with the bamboos and twine. Then it was simple to draw the patterns on the ground with the sand. For each knot I measured out an 8ft (2.44m) square, outlined it with twine, and marked the corners with bamboo canes. I left a 1ft (30cm) margin between the knots and the wall on either side. Knots 1 and 3, and 2 and 4, are positioned 3ft (90cm) apart, while 3 and 5, and 4 and 6, are 2ft (60cm) apart.

With more bamboos, I marked 2ft (60cm) intervals along the sides of each knot. Then I joined opposite canes with lengths of twine to make the grid on the ground, adding the diagonals for knots 3

and 4. Now I was ready to scribe the patterns and 'draw' them with sand.

To form the square within each knot, I drew a line in sand from the centre of each side to the centre of its adjacent sides.

For knots 1 and 2, I used my compass to scribe a semicircle of 2ft (60cm) radius from the centre of each side. I marked the semicircles and the corners of the knots with sand.

For knots 3 and 4, I drew a 2ft (60cm) square in the centre of each knot and an 18in (45cm) circle, centred on the diagonals, in each corner. I extended the lines of the centre square to join the outlines of the circles.

In the same way, using the grid lines as my guide, the compass to scribe the curves, and sand to mark the design, I drew patterns 5, 6 and 7 on the ground.

I had calculated approximately how many plants would be required, and I had brought them with me too (adding a few spares for safety): for each of knots 1 and 2, 100 plants of golden box and 60 plants of teucrium (wall germander); for each of knots 3 and 4, 120 plants of green box and 60 teucrium; for patterns 5 and 6, 80 golden box and two box balls each; for pattern 7, 100 green box; and six shaped green box plants for the trios of pyramids.

In calculating approximate numbers of plants required:

At 5in apart, seven plants are needed per yard run; using metric, at 12.5cm apart, eight are needed per metre run.

At 6in apart, six are needed per yard run; at 15cm apart, seven per metre run. As I laid out the designs my gardener planted the box and the teucrium 5in (13 cm) apart along the sand guidelines. The woven effect was created by placing the 'cross over' plant row so that it interrupted the 'cross under' row. We managed to complete the whole job in one day, the final touch being to spread the gravel between the threads of the knots.

Since then the plants have been kept beautifully clipped. They are trimmed twice a year, in early and late summer, with the 'cross over' plants allowed to grow taller so they appear to rise up and over the line 'beneath'. Now, eight years later, the knots still look immaculate.

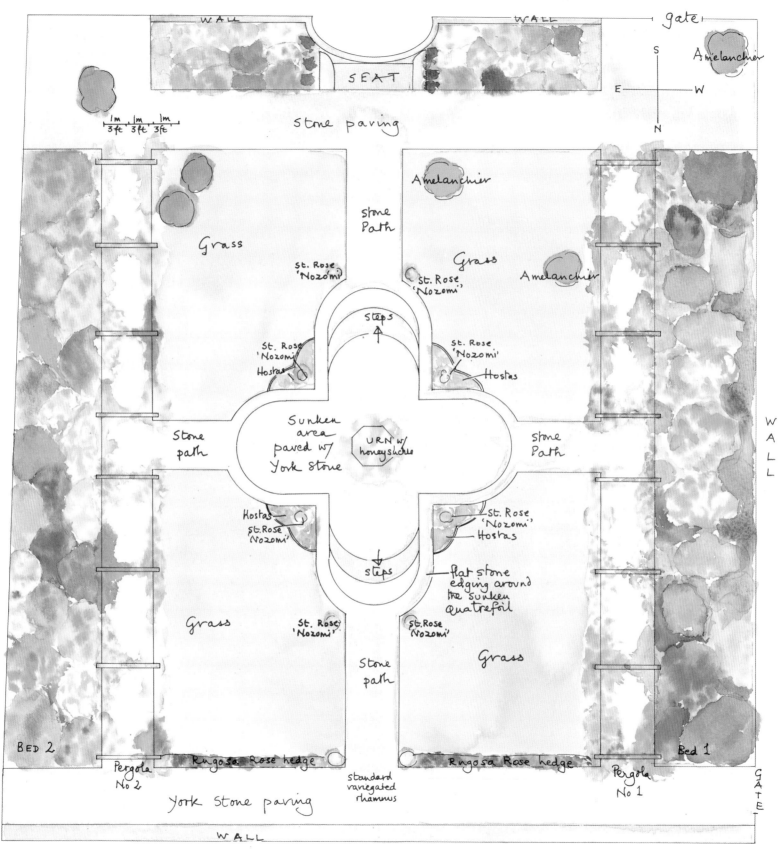

WALL   WALL   gate

SEAT

S
E ─── W
N

Amelanchier

1m 1m 1m
3ft 3ft 3ft

stone paving

stone
Path

Amelanchier

Grass

St. Rose
'Nozomi'

Grass

Amelanchier

St. Rose
'Nozomi'

Steps

St. Rose
'Nozomi'

Hostas

St. Rose
'Nozomi'

Hostas

Stone
path

Sunken
area
paved w/
York Stone

URN w/
honeysuckle

stone
Path

Hostas

St.Rose
'Nozomi'

St. Rose
'Nozomi'

Hostas

Steps

flat stone
edging around
the sunken
Quatrefoil

Grass

St. Rose
'Nozomi'

St.Rose
'Nozomi'

Grass

Stone
path

BED 2   Bed 1

Pergola
No 2

Rugosa Rose hedge

standard
variegated
rhamnus

Rugosa Rose hedge

Pergola
No 1

GATE

York stone paving

WALL

W
A
L
L

PERGOLAS IN A SECRET GARDEN

*A*BLINGTON IS A HAMLET *of Bibury, in Gloucestershire, further up the river Coln. According to an inscription on the porch, John Coxwell built the Manor in 1590. The house has a beautiful setting, with the main door on the south façade leading you on to a wide stone terrace, down a few steps, then along a gentle grass slope to the sparkling river, flowing 64m (70 yards) away. Beyond the river the densely wooded ground rises steeply, and here the owner, Robert Cooper, has planted a ribbon of daffodils which in spring erupts into a golden cascade.*

Above: *In the border behind the first pergola, grape hyacinths,* Puschkinia libanotica *and rich Barnhaven primulas create an early spring display, well timed to combine with the emerging peony shoots. This is the awakening moment of the year. From now on there will be an ever-changing palette of flower and leaf texture and colour.*

Right: *An overall view from the south-east corner of the walled garden – a quiet evening picture taken in early summer, just as the roses are coming into bloom. This carefully planned garden, with its planting at different levels, shows how verticals can be as important as horizontals in garden design.*

Immediately to the left of the house is a walled garden, originally used for vegetables. Here Robert wished to make a small secret garden, a quiet place to walk and relax in. He first approached me in the spring of 1983 and in the early autumn I wrote to him, 'The all-important wall garden is to be treated as your winter work and we will make it stunning.'

I drew up outline designs. The garden was to be formal, with York stone paths, and as Robert is fond of roses and clematis we decided to have two pergolas, running parallel to each other from north to south. As well as supporting climbers, they would provide the change of level which is so important when there is no outlook (this garden is enclosed on all four sides by Cotswold stone walls). Then I started to think about the central space. I always like to see if the house has any features that could be reflected in the garden, and here were typical Elizabethan gables, of a shape that could be modified and repeated to make a quatrefoil pattern for the centre. Robert did not want a pond – he already had the river – so we decided that the quatrefoil would be a sunken, paved area. Now it was a matter of getting the shapes and proportions right, and drawing the plan to scale so that the construction work could be done.

At this time Robert had two expert builders working for him and they constructed the pergolas using 15 x 15cm (6 x 6in) oak posts. There are eight pairs of pillars on each pergola, which adds up to thirty-two in all. They are 3.2m (10½ft) apart and the pathway between them is about 2m (7ft) wide.

Robert's letter of 7 January 1985 says, 'I would be very pleased if you could suggest clematis or roses that you think would blend with the colours of the peonies as I have arranged them, taking into consideration that whilst underplanting in the spring can be tulips, grape hyacinths, primroses or miniature narcissus, for underplanting to follow in summer and autumn

I do not have any particular ideas other than galtonias and foxgloves.'

Robert's peonies were put in, and I set about ordering the plants for the pergolas. I wanted sixteen roses and sixteen clematis for the first pergola – two climbers on each support. The colour scheme was to be basically pink and white, to blend with the peonies, and for extra interest I included a few blues and some purple. The second pergola was to have twelve roses (again pink and white), two honeysuckles and two

Right: Nepeta mussinii *embraces the feet of the solid oak pillars. This post is draped with rose 'Climbing Mme Caroline Testout' and* Clematis *'Lasurstern'.*

Below: *Robert Cooper chose and ordered a comprehensive selection of peonies, which are backed by delphiniums and lilies for summer display. The wall behind has climbing roses and vines.*

First Pergola

1 Rose 'Albertine', coppery pink
   Clematis macropetala 'Snowbird', no pruning

2 Rose 'New Dawn', blush pink
   Clematis 'Nelly Moser', mauve pink, dark bar,
   light prune

3 Rose 'Pink Perpétué', rose pink
   Clematis Mrs Cholmondeley', light blue,
   light prune

4 Rose 'Cupid', flesh pink
   Clematis 'William Kennett', lavender, light prune

5 Rose 'Dream Girl', pink
   Clematis 'Perle d'Azur', sky blue, hard prune

6 Rose 'Kathleen Harrop', clear pink
   Clematis 'Comtesse de Bouchaud', mauve pink,
   hard prune

7 Rose 'Blush Noisette', lilac pink
   Clematis 'Miss Bateman', cream, light prune

8 Rose 'Mme Alfred Carrière'
   white, tinted pink
   Clematis florida 'Sieboldii', white, purple centre,
   hard prune

9 Rose 'Mme Alfred Carrière'
   white, tinted pink
   Clematis viticella 'Alba Luxurians', creamy white,
   hard prune

10 Rose 'Aimée Vibert', white
   Clematis 'Hagley Hybrid', shell pink, light prune

11 Rose 'Félicité Perpétue', white with pale pink
   Clematis 'Edith', pure white, light prune

12 Rose 'Albéric Barbier', creamy white
   Clematis viticella 'Purpurea Plena Elegans'
   hard prune

13 Rose 'François Juranville', glowing pink
   Clematis 'Comtesse de Bouchaud',
   cyclamen pink, hard prune

14 Rose 'Compassion', pink
   Clematis 'Vyvyan Pennell', lavender, light prune

15 Rose 'Climbing Mme Caroline Testout', pink
   Clematis 'Lasurstern', rich blue, light prune

16 Rose 'Mme Grégoire Staechelin', cerise pink
   Clematis 'Walter Pennell' (dble), lilac pink,
   light prune

Left: *The theme of this pergola is pink and mauve.*
Clematis *'Hagley Hybrid'* (centre) *has pointed
shell-pink flowers in summer.* C. viticella
'Purpurea Plena Elegans' (bottom) *is breathtaking
when it flowers flamboyantly in late summer.*

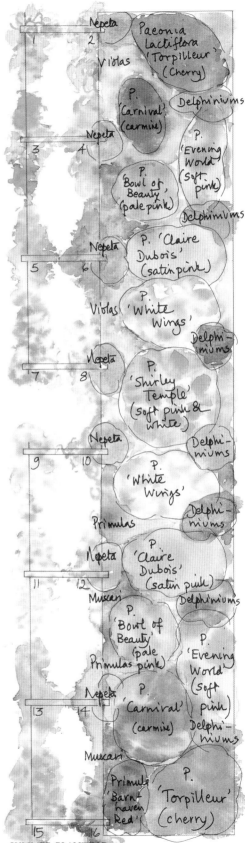

SUMMER PLANTING

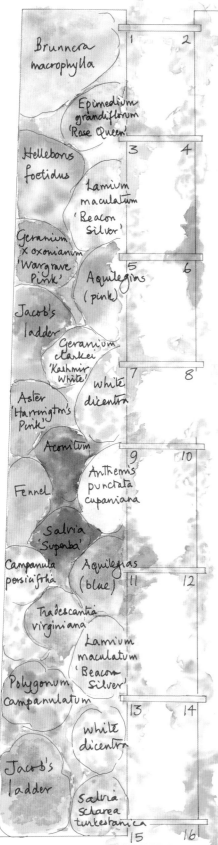

SECOND PERGOLA

1 Rose 'Wedding Day'
   apricot buds, opening
   white

2 Rose 'Albertine'
   coppery pink

3 *Lonicera* × *americana*

4 Rose 'Bobbie James'
   creamy white

5 Rose 'Aimée Vibert'
   white

6 *Vitis* 'Brant'
   autumn colour
   black grapes

7 Rose 'Climbing Mme Abel
   Chatenay'
   blush pink

8 Rose 'Handel'
   cream edged pink

9 *Vitis vinifera* 'Purpurea'

10 Rose 'Frances E. Lester'
   single white

11 Rose 'Pink Perpétué'
   rose pink

12 Rose 'Blush Noisette'
   lilac pink

13 *Lonicera japonica* var.
   repens
   cream and red

14 Rose 'Kiftsgate'
   creamy white

15 Rose 'Rambling Rector'
   creamy white

16 Rose 'Aloha'
   rich pink

Right: *Each rose is to be enjoyed for its intrinsic allure. 'Handel'* (top) *is a repeat-flowering climber. The legendary* Rosa filipes *'Kiftsgate'* (centre), *so spectacular growing up a big tree, still looks beautiful when restricted by pruning. Lovely 'Aloha'* (bottom), *a small climber with a delightful fragrance, flowers all summer long.*

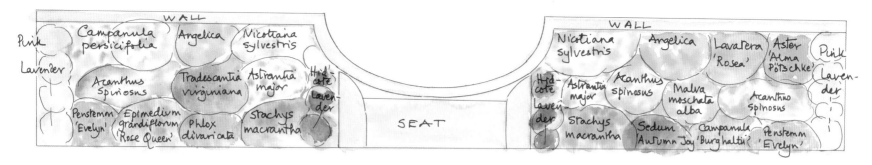

WALL · WALL

Pink Lavender · Campanula persicifolia · Angelica · Nicottana sylvestris · Acanthus spinosus · Tradescantia virginiana · Astrantia major · Penstemon 'Evelyn' · Epimedium grandiflorum 'Rose Queen' · Phlox divaricata · Stachys macrantha · Hidcote Lavender

Nicotiana sylvestris · Angelica · Lavatera 'Rosea' · Aster 'Alma Pötschke' · Pink Lavender · Hidcote Lavender · Astrantia major · Acanthus spinosus · Malva moschata alba · Acanthus spinosus · Stachys macrantha · Sedum 'Autumn Joy' · Campanula 'Burghaltii' · Penstemon 'Evelyn' · SEAT

SUMMER PLANTING

vines, one up each pillar. It was quite a time-consuming exercise finding them all. This is where the designer feels frustrated: you telephone a nursery and get a positive response to your list of requests, and then two days later a message comes saying several are not available, and you start once more almost at square one. For my twenty-eight roses, sixteen clematis, two honeysuckles and two vines I had to go to four nurseries. Then, whose side are you on when the owner writes that '*Clematis* 'Perle d'Azur' is dead and, according to my gardener, arrived so'? The hazards of a go-between ... But none of these things matter if one is determined to make the garden the best ever.

I enjoy designing with an owner who makes constructive suggestions. Robert's peonies are the backbone of the border behind the first pergola and now every spring they look dramatic. They are followed in summer by *Allium christophii* and delphiniums, lilies, galtonias and foxgloves, with climbing roses on the wall behind.

Robert gave me two packets of Barnhaven primula seed for which I will always be grateful. I passed on to him all the seedlings of the first germination. They look wonderful in early spring, beside the young shoots of the peonies. But we did not discard the seed tray: slowly a second germination of these lovely primulas came through and I have them in my own garden, associating with a dwarf pink prunus and *Primula* 'Wanda'.

The border by the second pergola is rather a shady place, but I persisted with my favourite perennials, and they have done well. Our aim is to have a succession of bloom from spring through to autumn. Hellebores are always exciting in late winter, lamiums, epimediums and hardy geraniums offer anticipation in spring, and there are salvias, Jacob's ladder, aquilegias and tradescantias for summer.

As you walk into this garden from the gate in the north-west corner, there is a rose walk with a hedge of Rugosa roses on your right, and on the left, under the south-facing wall, are roses that Robert has moved from elsewhere. The theme again is pink and white, with 'Fantin Latour' and 'Nozomi' blending perfectly with the planting on the pergolas and in the borders. At the opposite end of the garden is an elegant sixteenth-century stone seat. On either side is a small bed planted with lavender and perennials.

A garden without some green space is unthinkable. Grass is cool in the summer and comforting in the winter, and is a great coordinator. So we made four small lawns around the sunken area. Each of the inside corners has a standard rose 'Nozomi', underplanted with a variety of hostas, all looking healthy.

As a finishing touch, Robert placed at the centre of the quatrefoil an octagonal lead urn that overflows with honeysuckle. It adds a further dignity to this increasingly beautiful walled garden.

Every garden must have a seat to relax in. From this beautiful sixteenth-century seat, surrounded by scented plants, there is a view of the whole garden.

RIBBON BORDERS

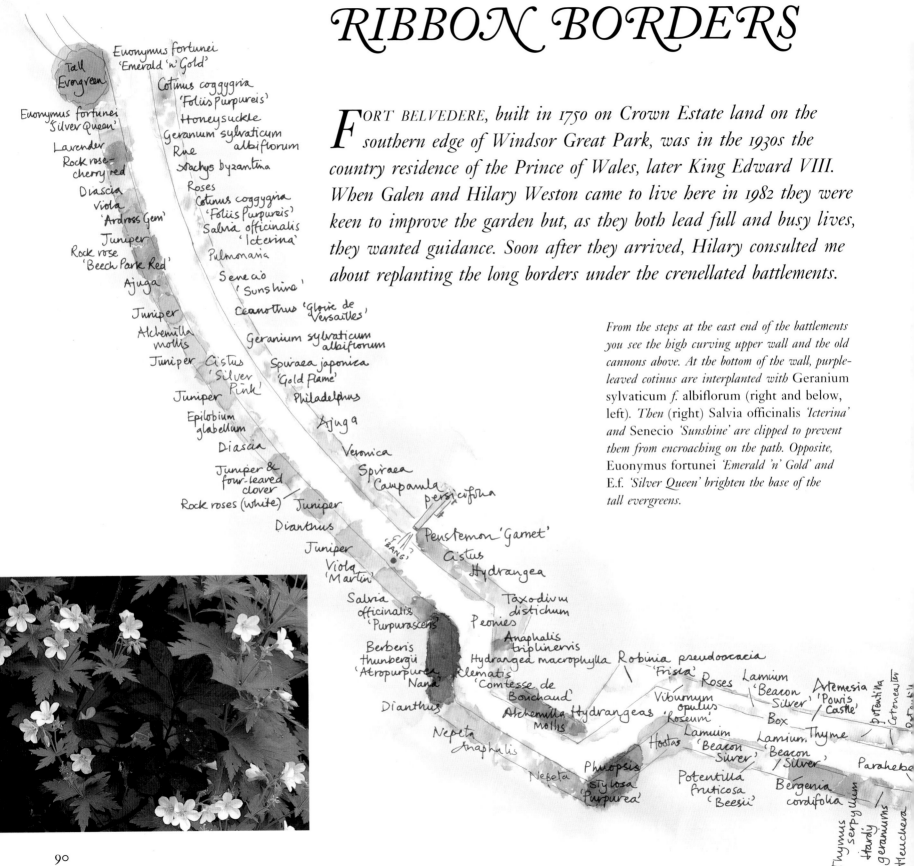

*F*ORT BELVEDERE, *built in 1750 on Crown Estate land on the southern edge of Windsor Great Park, was in the 1930s the country residence of the Prince of Wales, later King Edward VIII. When Galen and Hilary Weston came to live here in 1982 they were keen to improve the garden but, as they both lead full and busy lives, they wanted guidance. Soon after they arrived, Hilary consulted me about replanting the long borders under the crenellated battlements.*

From the steps at the east end of the battlements you see the high curving upper wall and the old cannons above. At the bottom of the wall, purple-leaved cotinus are interplanted with Geranium sylvaticum *f.* albiflorum (right and below, left). *Then* (right) Salvia officinalis *'Icterina' and* Senecio *'Sunshine' are clipped to prevent them from encroaching on the path. Opposite,* Euonymus fortunei *'Emerald 'n' Gold' and* E.f. *'Silver Queen' brighten the base of the tall evergreens.*

Tall Evergreen
Euonymus fortunei 'Emerald 'n' Gold'
Euonymus fortunei 'Silver Queen'
Cotinus coggygria 'Foliis Purpureis'
Lavender
Honeysuckle
Rock rose – cherry red
Geranium sylvaticum albiflorum
Rue
Diascia
Stachys byzantina
viola 'Ardross Gem'
Roses
Cotinus coggygria 'Foliis Purpureis'
Juniper
Salvia officinalis 'Icterina'
Rock rose 'Beech Park Red'
Pulmonaria
Ajuga
Senecio 'Sunshine'
Juniper
Ceanothus 'Gloire de Versailles'
Alchemilla mollis
Geranium sylvaticum albiflorum
Juniper Cistus 'Silver Pink'
Spiraea japonica 'Gold Flame'
Juniper
Philadelphus
Epilobium glabellum
Ajuga
Diascia
Veronica
Juniper & four-leaved clover
Spiraea
Rock roses (white) Juniper
Campanula persicifolia
Dianthus
Juniper
Penstemon 'Garnet'
Viola 'Martin'
'BANG'
Cistus
Hydrangea
Salvia officinalis 'Purpurascens'
Taxodium distichum
Peonies
Berberis thunbergii 'Atropurpurea' Nana
Anaphalis triplinervis
Hydrangea macrophylla
Robinia pseudoacacia 'Frisia'
Roses
Lamium 'Beacon Silver'
Artemisia 'Powis Castle'
Clematis 'Comtesse de Bouchaud'
Viburnum opulus 'Roseum'
Box
Dianthus
Alchemilla mollis
Hydrangeas
Lamium 'Beacon Silver'
Thyme
Nepeta
Hostas
Lamium 'Beacon Silver'
Parahebe
Anaphalis
Phuopsis stylosa
Potentilla fruticosa 'Beesii'
Bergenia cordifolia
Nepeta 'Purpurea'
Thymus serpyllum
hardy geraniums
Heuchera
Potentilla
Cotoneaster

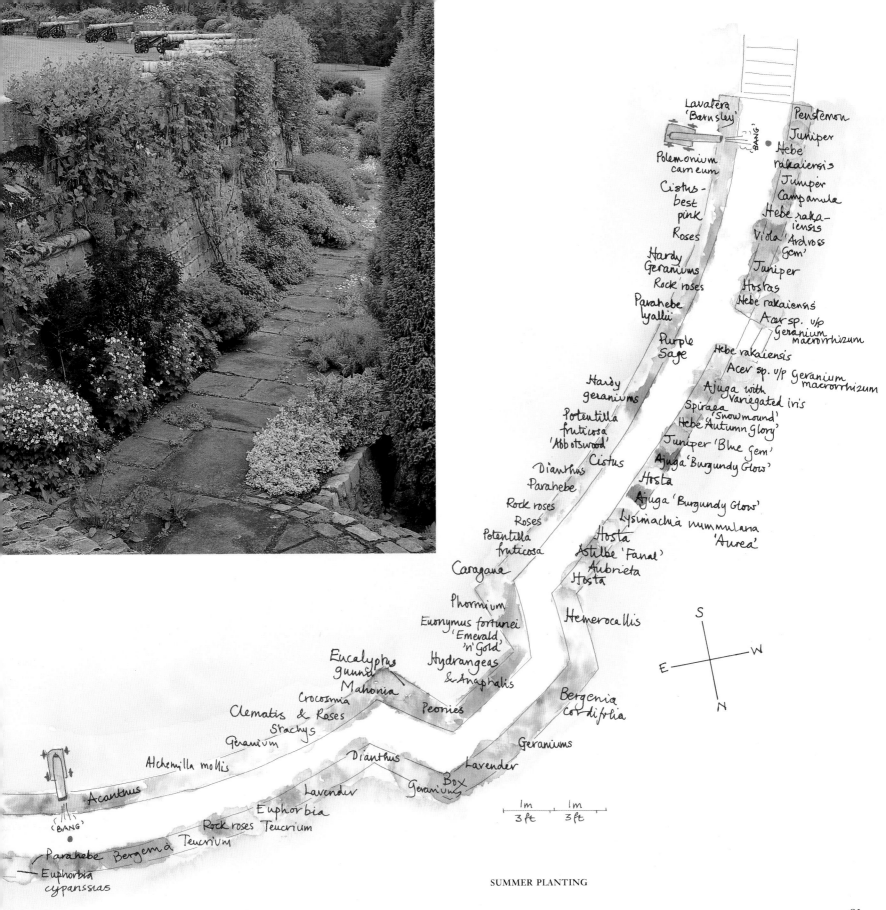

Lavatera
'Barnsley'   Penstemon
                                        Juniper
Polemonium   Hebe
carneum   rakaiensis
                                        Juniper
Cistus -   Campanula
best
pink   Hebe rakai-
Roses   ensis
                                        Viola 'Ardross
Hardy   Gem'
Geraniums
Rock roses   Juniper
Parahebe   Hostas
lyallii   Hebe rakaiensis
                                        Acer sp. v/p
Purple   Geranium
Sage   macrorrhizum

        Hardy   Hebe rakaiensis
        geraniums   Acer sp. v/p Geranium
                                             macrorrhizum
        Potentilla   Ajuga with
        fruticosa   variegated iris
        'Abbotswood'   Spiraea
                                'Snowmound'
                                Hebe 'Autumn Glory'
              Dianthus   Cistus Juniper 'Blue Gem'
              Parahebe   Ajuga 'Burgundy Glow'
              Rock roses   Hosta
              Roses   Ajuga 'Burgundy Glow'
              Potentilla   Lysimachia nummularia
              fruticosa   'Aurea'
                                Hosta
        Caragana   Astilbe 'Fanal'
                          Aubrieta
                          Hosta

        Phormium
        Euonymus fortunei   Hemerocallis
        'Emerald'
        'n' Gold'
Eucalyptus   Hydrangeas
gunnii   & Anaphalis
    Mahonia   Bergenia
Crocosmia   cordifolia
Clematis & Roses   Peonies
    Stachys
Geranium   Geraniums
Alchemilla mollis   Lavender
             Dianthus   Box
Acanthus   Geraniums
       Lavender
    Euphorbia
Rock roses Teucrium

Parahebe Bergenia Teucrium

Euphorbia
cyparissias

(BANG)

S
E ✛ W
  N

1m   1m
3ft   3ft

SUMMER PLANTING

91

The grey-green leaves and fluffy white flower heads of Anaphalis triplinervis *contrast with deep pink* Hydrangea macrophylla.

Opposite: *The path leads you between narrow beds. In the border at the top of the low retaining wall,* Berberis thunbergii *'Atropurpurea Nana' and purple sage form good mounds, as does the golden sage that has been added to the planting. On the other side, hydrangeas make a great summer display in association with* Clematis *'Comtesse de Bouchaud'. The tall evergreens mark the eastern end of the borders. Notice how well the climbers have grown – they now reach up and over the wall.*

Few of us have such a dramatic setting to care for. However, many garden owners have a narrow border under a wall, and much the same basic requirement as Galen and Hilary – that when they are strolling or sitting in the garden in the evening they should have the pleasure of interesting planting, with colour and scent.

Walking along these borders for the first time, I felt they went on for ever. They are actually just over 110m (120 yards), and as they are curved in a slightly flattened convex semicircle you can see at most one third at a time. From the lawn beside the Fort there is a 4m (13ft) drop down to the lower lawn. The fall is cleverly designed. First there is a 3m (10ft) retaining wall with a bed 75cm (30in) wide underneath it. Then comes a stone path with plenty of pockets for planting, then another narrow bed (this one just 50cm/20in wide), then a further retaining wall 1m (39in) high. These ribbon beds and the climbers and wall shrubs – mostly roses, ceanothus, clematis and honeysuckles – have been tended since the 1960s, with the utmost skill, by Tony, the Lithuanian gardener. I was called in to increase the repertoire of plants and discard the less exciting ones.

One good thing was that the water drained from the lawn above the high wall into these beds, so they were always moist but never too wet. A bad point was that the soil was tired and needed total digging and feeding, but this would not be too difficult to remedy.

Tony knew that he could not take on this job in addition to his other commitments, so contractors were brought in. They started at the eastern end, which had been completely taken over by the pink everlasting pea: it looked pretty enough while in flower, but smothered everything else. The contractors then worked along the borders, taking out unwanted specimens but leaving mature clumps of peonies, wonderful hydrangeas, acanthus, daylilies, bergenias and hypericums. They also

Above: *Attractive foliage can play an important role all through the year. The clipped box ball contrasts well in colour, shape and texture with* Lamium maculatum *'Beacon Silver' and the grey filigree leaves of* Artemisia *'Powis Castle'*.

Left: Phuopsis stylosa *'Purpurea' makes a dense ground cover most of the year but dies back in winter. The dark form of the Irish weed is much better than the more usual paler version. When the foliage is damp it has a strong smell of foxes.*

pruned the shrubs on the high wall, and this is where I made an error. The climbing roses and clematis had become leggy enough to top the wall, and I suggested that they should all be severely cut back. Too late I realized that they had been allowed to behave like this so that they would flower through the crenellations on top of the wall and so be seen from the house. Eventually all was well: they now flower on strong new growth up and over the wall, visible from both sides, so the pruning ultimately improved them.

When it came to new planting, my thoughts were to include enough ground cover and low evergreens to maintain winter interest. (Once I realized that I was also keeping the deer and rabbits well fed in the cold months, I took Tony's advice and agreed that the tastiest, most tender greens should be covered with netting.) All the plants I chose were fairly easy. There were ajugas, dianthus, nepeta, rock roses, anaphalis, veronicas, violas, *Epilobium glabellum*, pulmonarias, and four-leaved clover, with lots of others. The borders, being long and narrow, required planting strips of at least 1.8m (6ft) to create an impact. On the high wall side of the path we were able to have taller plants, and in corners made by the 'look-outs' we planted *Taxodium distichum*, *Robinia pseudoacacia* 'Frisia' and *Eucalyptus gunnii*, knowing that one day their heads would appear over the wall.

Just as everything was filling out and Tony was keeping the deer and rabbits at bay, the high wall ran into trouble. Much of it required repointing. This meant that precautions were necessary, to prevent the plants in the borders from being smothered with old mortar dust. The climbers were laid flat, and they and the larger shrubs were given protective coverings. Tony dug up all he could and put the plants in a waiting ground, to be returned as the work proceeded. At least we had found out by then what the rabbits

The beauty of the guelder rose, Viburnum opulus 'Roseum', *is at its peak even before the snowballs form the dazzling white display shown here* (above). *The flowers start in spring as an alluring chartreuse colour, wonderful underplanted with blue muscari or palest yellow primroses. They echo the colour of* Euphorbia cyparissias (right). Alchemilla mollis *and white and yellow potentillas contribute to the yellow and white theme – though the red heuchera that has crept in is something of a distraction!*

Above: *This section of the borders, towards the western end, has largely been replanted. Now there is mixed planting of hydrangeas, peonies, potentillas, hardy geraniums, anaphalis and stachys under the high wall. In the foreground are* Bergenia cordifolia, *hardy geraniums and two box shapes. Beyond are dianthus, lavender and wall germander.*

Right: *A long-standing planting of the old-fashioned montbretia has spread into a 3m (10ft) ribbon under the high wall. It now goes under the name of crocosmia and comes in new, improved forms, with flowers that are larger, more upstanding, and range in colour from soft yellow through orange to bright reds.*

Opposite, above: *Under the high wall is a selection of potentillas and cistus, underplanted with parahebe, dianthus and rock roses. In the foreground, on the low retaining wall, clipped box is among hostas, golden-leaved creeping jenny, astilbe and, finally, a long planting of hemerocallis (daylilies).*

Opposite, below: *Steps from these borders down to the swimming pool are flanked by Japanese maples underplanted with* Geranium macrorrhizum. *The box shapes are an addition to the original planting plan.*

liked, and we were able to concentrate on what they found less palatable. I also had the opportunity to put in a few more plants under the high wall – more white potentilla, *Lavatera* 'Barnsley', *Artemisia* 'Powis Castle' and our own cistus, the one that we at Barnsley call 'best pink'. I grew this from seed collected from a Corsican cistus.

Today these borders, having been very well cared for, look remarkably full and luxuriant. Walking along the path you see a continuous stream of colour, leaf shape and texture, punctuated by the outlines of well-tended shrubs. The walls are covered, not only with roses, clematis, honeysuckles and ceanothus, but also by campanulas, aubrieta, moss, sedums and snow-on-the-mountain, sprouting from the crevices. Although I did not have a definite colour scheme in mind, all the blues, pinks and reds blend well together, with splashes of gold for brightness, and grey to complete the picture. I hope that winter has shape and form, spring provides an explosion of interest, and summer and autumn have coordination of colour.

A DROUGHT-TOLERANT KNOT GARDEN

AFTER A VISIT to Jacksonville, Florida, when I spoke about garden design, I was invited by a member of the Garden Club to suggest some ideas to improve the view from their clubhouse, looking towards the river.

Agapanthus *'Ardernei Hybrid' loves sunshine and thrives in well-drained soil.*

The clubhouse looked out on a grassy area 44m (48 yards) long by 20m (22 yards) wide, interspersed with a muddled planting of day-lilies (hemerocallis), tired roses and mature hollies, unintended annuals, and sprawling plants which had no right to be there.

On either side of this was the asphalt-surfaced park, each car space defined by concrete headers – a clever idea to keep the parking disciplined, but now it all looked untidy as weeds had strayed into the asphalt, so the definition had been lost.

Having strong ideas about aesthetics is certainly one aspect of garden design, but it is also essential to consult local conditions – not to mention the requirements of the client. In this case there were quite strict limitations, some imposed by the climate, others by club regulations. The asphalt car park had to be kept, there was no possibility of planting trees for shade, and there was no irrigation system. My proposed planting (down the central strip) must consist of drought-tolerant shrubs and plants which would survive, not only the bright sunlight and very high temperatures of the Florida summer, but also occasional winter frosts. There was an additional restriction on plant height, which had to be kept low so the view towards and over the river was not obstructed. I did not question the

The exotic Hibiscus rosa-sinensis *has dramatic blooms throughout the summer.*

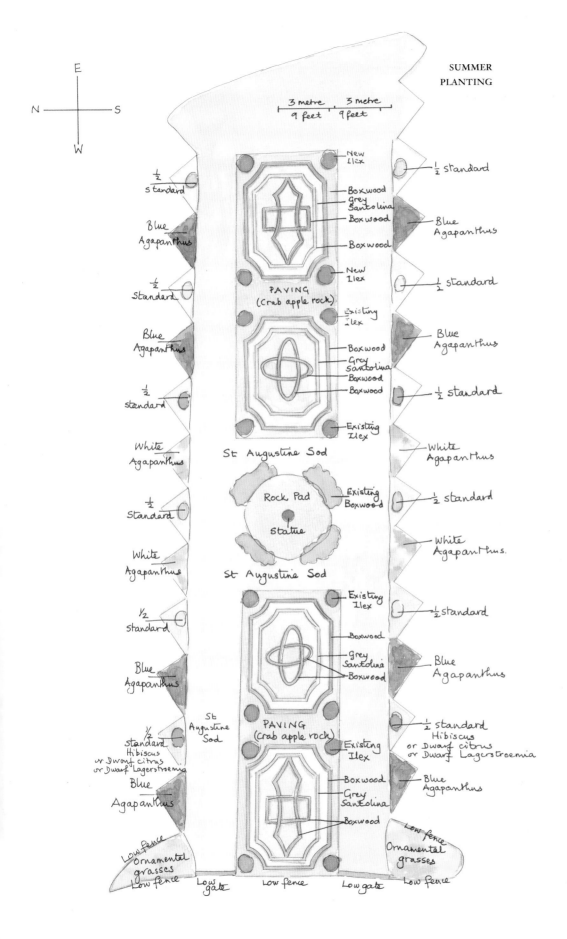

E
N —— S
W

3 metre | 3 metre
9 feet | 9 feet

New Ilex

½ standard

½ standard

Boxwood
Grey Santolina
Boxwood

Blue Agapanthus

Blue Agapanthus

Boxwood

New Ilex

½ standard

PAVING
(crab apple rock)

Existing Ilex

Blue Agapanthus

Boxwood
Grey santolina
Boxwood
Boxwood

Blue Agapanthus

½ standard

Standard

½ standard

Blue Agapanthus

White Agapanthus

St Augustine Sod

Existing Ilex

White Agapanthus

½ standard

½ standard

Existing Boxwood

Rock Pad

Statue

½ standard

White Agapanthus

St Augustine Sod

White Agapanthus

Standard

½ standard

Existing Ilex

½ standard

Blue Agapanthus

Boxwood
Grey Santolina
Boxwood

Blue Agapanthus

St Augustine Sod

½ standard
standard Hibiscus
or Dwarf citrus
or Dwarf Lagerstroemia

PAVING
(crab apple rock)

½ standard
Hibiscus
or Dwarf citrus
or Dwarf Lagerstroemia

Existing Ilex

Blue Agapanthus

Boxwood
Grey SanEolina

Blue Agapanthus

Boxwood

Low Fence
Ornamental grasses
Low Fence

Low Fence
Ornamental grasses

Low gate

Low fence

Low gate

Low Fence

height or colour of the cars – my only stipulation was that their exhausts should not blow directly on to my new planting!

My approach was practical. I had been told that the garden should be easy to maintain. With a formal design, a team could be brought in to tidy and clip. They would be given precise instructions and would not require much horticultural knowledge. On the other hand, if I provided a plan with mixed planting, the gardener would need to have a sensitive approach and a detailed knowledge of plants. Once I started to think in these terms, the decision was clear. Moreover, looking down from the clubhouse, it was evident that a formal design would not only provide the most practical solution, but would also be the most satisfying aesthetically.

I sat down with my paper and rule and scribbled some geometric patterns to run the length of the area. I had been glad to consult local knowledge about plants which would do well. Remembering also that they should not obstruct the view, I chose low-growing box, santolina and dwarf hollies to create the patterns. I included the existing hollies among the markers on the corners of the knot patterns.

Along each side, fitting into the triangles created by the concrete headers, I suggested using half-standard hibiscus, citrus and dwarf lagerstroemia to give colour and sufficient but not too much height. These would be in alternate triangles, and would be surrounded with gravel. The remaining triangles would be filled with blocks of white and blue agapanthus, for more colour. The grass on each side of the knots would be St Augustine sod (*Stenotaphrum secundatum*), which withstands the Florida climate. A decorative fence and two low gates would define the end near the clubhouse and would prevent cars encroaching on the lawn.

With only a little basic maintenance, this design would remain immaculate, and would provide interest throughout the year.

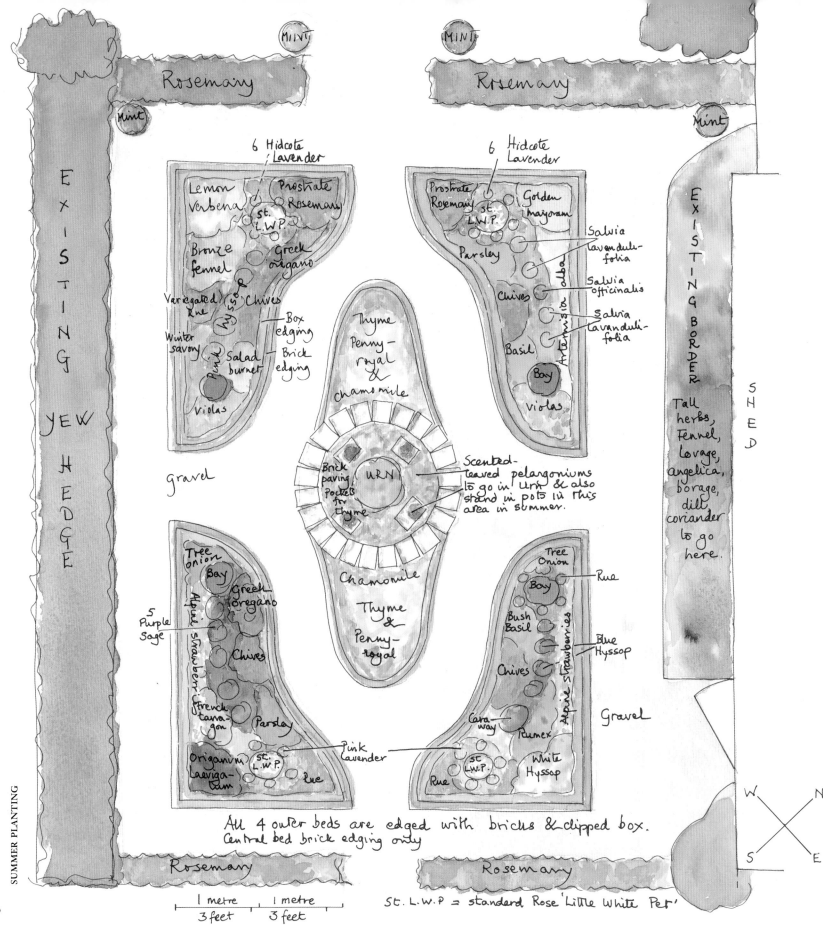

MINT

Rosemary

MINT

MINT

Rosemary

MINT

E X I S T I N G Y E W H E D G E

E X I S T I N G B O R D E R

S H E D

6 Hidcote Lavender

Lemon Verbena

Prostrate Rosemary

St. L.W.P.

Bronze fennel

Greek oregano

Variegated Rue

Hyssop

Chives

Box edging

Brick edging

Winter savory

Pink

Salad burner

Violas

6 Hidcote Lavender

Prostrate Rosemary

St. L.W.P.

Golden marjoram

Parsley

Salvia lavandulifolia

Salvia officinalis

Chives

Artemisia alba

Salvia lavandulifolia

Basil

Bay

Violas

Gravel

Thyme Penny-royal & chamomile

Brick paving pockets for thyme

URN

Scented-leaved pelargoniums to go in urn & also stand in pots in this area in summer.

Chamomile Thyme & Penny-royal

Tree onion

Bay

Greek oregano

Alpine strawberries

5 Purple Sage

Chives

French tarragon

Parsley

Origanum Laevigatum

St. L.W.P.

Rue

Pink Lavender

Tall herbs, Fennel, Lovage, angelica, borage, dill, coriander to go here.

Tree onion

Bay

Rue

Bush Basil

Alpine strawberries

Blue Hyssop

Chives

Cara-way

Rumex

White Hyssop

Rue

St. L.W.P.

Gravel

All 4 outer beds are edged with bricks & clipped box. Central bed brick edging only

W N
S E

1 metre | 1 metre
3 feet | 3 feet

St. L.W.P = standard Rose 'Little White Pet'

A FORMAL HERB GARDEN

SOMETIMES A DEMANDING challenge produces an especially rewarding result. Marie-Christine de Laubarède and Prince Pierre d'Arenberg had been to Barnsley and enjoyed the garden, and later they invited me to visit Marie-Christine's home at Lime Close in Berkshire. I found there a truly wonderful garden which she had inherited from her aunt, Miss Cecilia Christie-Miller, a keen collector of alpines, bulbs and shrubs.

Above: *Just inside the box edging, rue encircles a bay tree, providing a contrast in leaf shape, texture and colour. A stray plant of* Viola labradorica *contributes its small purple flowers and heart-shaped dark leaves.*

Right: *The rectangular site at Lime Close demanded symmetry and scent. The outer beds, edged with brick and box, are filled with herbs for cooking and to dry for pot-pourri. Each has a standard rose 'Little White Pet', to add height. Low-growing herbs – thymes, pennyroyal and chamomile – occupy the curved beds on either side of the paved area surrounding the central urn.*

I felt how exciting it must be for Marie-Christine to become the owner of all these unusual plants, but I thought there was just one thing missing. I casually remarked, as we walked back to the house, 'You must have a herb garden here.'

Next there came a telephone call from the Prince, telling me that he wished to give Marie-Christine a herb garden as a surprise, and asking me if I would design and install it for her. Then came the punch line. She was going to be away for a week, starting from next Friday, and he would like the garden to be finished when she came back. This was Saturday. He suggested that I should come over to survey on Tuesday

and that work could start on the Friday. I took a deep breath. Well, why not, as long as John Hill of Sherborne Gardens was prepared to drop everything else for a week.

John was willing, and on Tuesday we went over to Lime Close to measure up. I contemplated while John took soil samples and excavated below the existing gravel. Much stony soil would have to be removed and replaced with topsoil.

The area available for the herb garden was a rectangle, enclosed on three sides by an existing 1.2m (4ft) yew hedge, the house and some stone outbuildings. The fourth side, near the greenhouse, was open, and I decided that here there should be a low rosemary hedge with a central opening. So I had my overall outline.

I planned out four symmetrical beds, each three-sided, two sides being straight and the third and longest a gentle curve. This left me with the central area, long and fairly narrow. An urn from elsewhere in the garden would make a good feature here. (I always look for existing garden features that might be used to greater advantage.) It could be surrounded with a circle of brick

Above: *Borage,* Borago officinalis, *is an annual, easily grown from seed. In rich soil it will easily reach a height of 1m (39in). The star-shaped blue flowers, with black anthers, are delightful as an addition to a salad, or floating in a summer drink.*

Below, left: *Aromatic hyssop,* Hyssopus officinalis, *is a perennial for a sunny spot.* Below, centre: *Coriander,* Coriandrum sativum, *in bloom at midsummer.* Below, right: *Parsley, with sage and chives.*

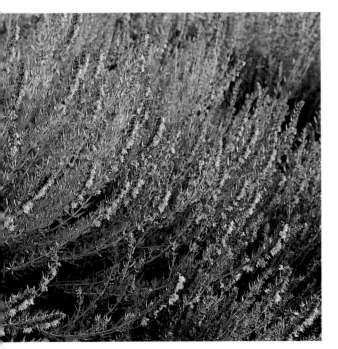

paving, with pockets left for thyme.

On either side of this central feature there would be space for two more beds (their final shape was decided by the width of the paths). The planting here should be kept to low-growing herbs – chamomile, pennyroyal and a variety of thymes.

In deciding on the planting in general, my aim was to give Marie-Christine as wide a selection as possible of culinary herbs, and also plants with sweet-smelling leaves and flowers to dry for pot-pourri.

John's men started preparing the ground on Friday, they worked through Saturday, and by Tuesday, a week to the day after our first survey, loads of topsoil were arriving and we were bringing in plants. In laying out the garden we kept very much to my original plan – there was no time to make alterations. The intention was that when Marie-Christine first saw the garden it would look as if it had been there for years, not days, so we used old bricks for the edging to the beds, and all the plants were as mature as possible.

It was a fast-moving adventure for us and a wonderful surprise for Marie-Christine.

Above: *Garden chives*, Allium schoenoprasum, *with their round purplish-pink flower heads, are one of the prettiest edgings for a herb bed. The leaves have a delicate onion flavour. Chopped, they make a subtle flavouring for salads and sauces.*

Below, left: *Rosemary*, Rosmarinus officinalis, *in full flower.* Below, centre: *The fresh green leaves of sorrel*, Rumex scutatus. Below, right: *Annual dill*, Anethum graveolens, *has yellow flowers followed by light winged seeds.*

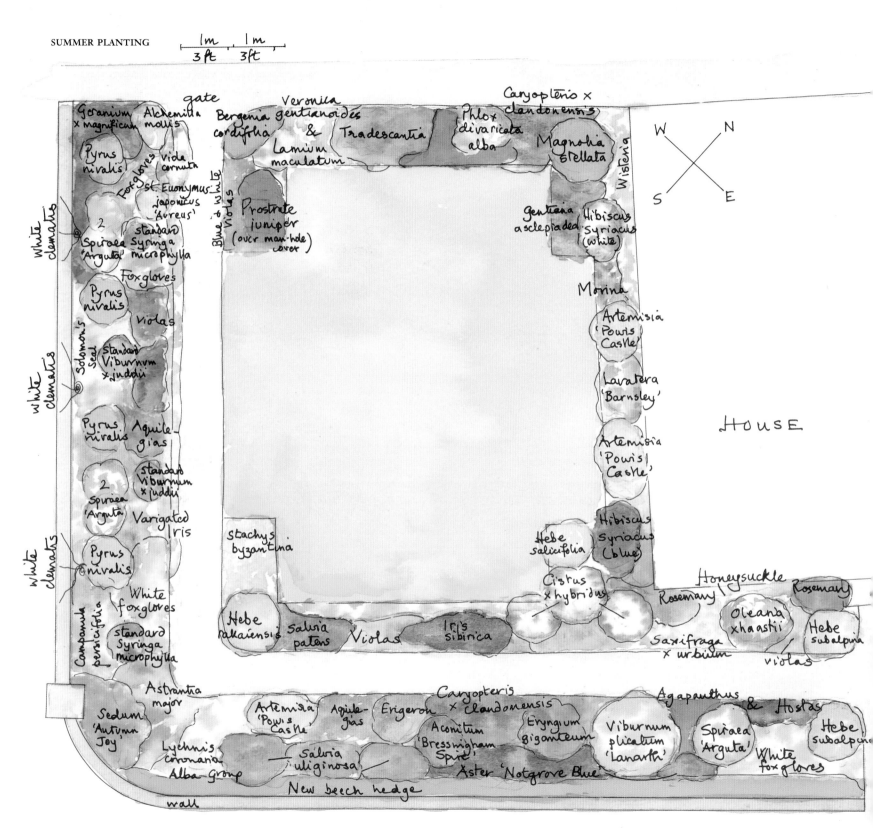

1m 1m
3ft 3ft

gate
Veronica
Geranium   Alchemilla   Bergenia   gentianoides   Caryopteris x
x magnificum   mollis   cordifolia   &   Tradescantia   Phlox   clandonensis
divaricata
Pyrus   viola   Lamium   alba   Magnolia
nivalis   Foxgloves   cornuta   maculatum   stellata
St. Euonymus   Wisteria
W   N
japonicus
'Aureus'   Blue Violas   Prostrate   Gentiana   Hibiscus
2   standard   juniper   asclepiadea   Syriacus   S   E
Spiraea   Syringa   (over man-hole   (white)
White clematis   'Arguta'   microphylla   cover)
Foxgloves   Morina
Pyrus   Artemisia
nivalis   Violas   'Powis
Castle'
Solomons   Lavatera
Seal   standard   'Barnsley'
White clematis   Viburnum   Artemisia
x juddii   'Powis
Pyrus   Aquile-   Castle'
nivalis   gias
standard   Hibiscus
2   Viburnum   Stachys   Hebe   Syriacus
Spiraea   x juddii   byzantina   salicifolia   (blue)
'Arguta'   Varigated
White clematis   Iris   Honeysuckle
Pyrus   Cistus   Rosemary   Rosemary
nivalis   x hybridus
White   Hebe   Salvia   Iris   Oleana   Hebe
Campanula persicifolia   foxgloves   rakaiensis   patens   Violas   sibirica   xhaastii   subalpina
standard   Saxifraga
Syringa   x urbium
microphylla   violas
Astrantia   Caryopteris x clandonensis   Agapanthus
major   Artemisia   Aquile-   Erigeron   & Hostas
Sedum   'Powis   gias   Eryngium   Viburnum
'Autumn   Castle'   Aconitum   giganteum   plicatum   Spiraea   Hebe
Joy'   'Bressingham   'Lanarth'   'Arguta'   subalpina
Lychnis   Salvia   Spire'   White
coronaria   uliginosa   foxgloves
Alba Group   Aster 'Notgrove Blue'
New beech hedge
wall

HOUSE

A MINIMUM UPKEEP GARDEN

WHEN I WAS asked to plan a garden for the Little House Farmhouse, Barnsley, my brief was that it should be simple in design and, while having plenty of flowers, be easy to maintain. For privacy, there must be a screen of trees along the wall adjoining the next garden.

In a corner of the border at the Little House Farmhouse, spring-flowering Spiraea *'Arguta' is underplanted by* Hosta sieboldiana *var.* elegans, *with handsome leaves that are bold and dramatic all through the summer.*

Arthur is out-walking with the dog whilst Catharine enjoys her garden.

Climbing rose

Rosemary

Deutzia

Pyrus salicifolia 'Pendula'

Varigated Iris

Hebe balpina

Lychnis Coronaria Alba Group

Philadelphus 'Belle Etoile'

Pyrus salicifolia 'Pendula'

Hebe Subalpina

Potentilla 'Vilmoriniana'

Asters (blue)

Hebe 'Blue Gem'

Philadelphus 'Belle Etoile'

Beech hedge

Wall

The shape was straightforward. There were narrow beds beside the house and surrounding the new lawn, then a path, then perimeter beds. We decided that the colours should be kept to blue and white, with a certain amount of grey – and, of course, green – as a background. Shrubs mixed with herbaceous and ground-cover plants would give a firm structure.

There was much discussion about the choice of trees to act as a screen along the north-facing wall. They must not grow too tall but they should have as much seasonal interest as possible, and an attractive shape, preferably more upright than spreading. We considered flowering cherries, malus, sorbus. The final choice, which I believe has proved a good one, is *Pyrus nivalis*, the snow pear. This tree is very beautiful early in the year, with pure white leaves and masses of flowers, and in autumn it has yellowish-green fruits. In front of the pears are two *Syringa microphylla* and two *Viburnum × juddii* (all standards), and there is an infilling of *Spiraea* 'Arguta' and white perennials.

There is always a decision to make, when using blue flowers, about how far you veer towards mauve. I tried to keep the blues as pure as possible, using tradescantia, a true blue aster, *Aconitum* 'Bressingham Spire' and, one of my favourite blues, *Salvia patens*. The aquilegias, which have seeded themselves in abundance, may be on the borderline of blue, but they are real cottage plants and I could not leave them out. There are lovely paler blues, including *Viola cornuta* and the autumn-flowering *Salvia uliginosa*.

The whites were easy to choose. We had to have a magnolia. For shrubs, as well as the spiraea and *Viburnum* × *juddii*, we decided on *V. plicatum* 'Lanarth', *Cistus* × *hybridus*, *Olearia* × *haastii*, with several hebes for their well-rounded shape.

In the border under the house, which faces almost due south, we put blue and white hibiscus, *Artemisia* 'Powis Castle' and *Lavatera* 'Barnsley' (hoping it would not go too pink). The roses on this wall are white, and so is the wisteria.

This simple garden, with its narrow beds and square lawn, suits the house well. The upkeep needed is minimal. It is already a lovely place to sit in the summer, and when the new beech hedge we planted five years ago grows tall, it will become a little secret garden.

Below: Salvia patens, *a wonderful strong blue, makes an important feature in summer and autumn borders. We treat it as an annual, sowing the seed in spring.*

Left: *Just inside the gate, white foxgloves are surrounded by* Alchemilla mollis *and* Viola cornuta alba, *and stand out sharply against the intense violet-blue flowers of* Geranium × magnificum.

Above: *The three-petalled flowers of tradescantia, the hardy spiderwort, seen from above.*

Below: *The delicate petals and vivid stamens of* Cistus × hybridus *have great charm.*

A CUTTING GARDEN

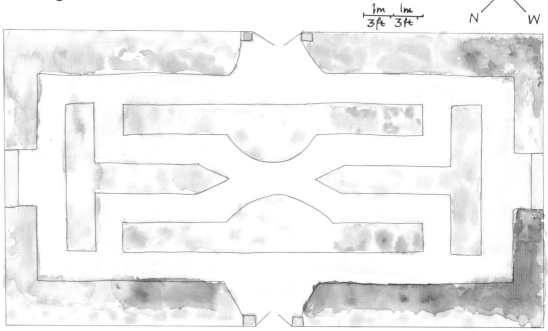

E S

N W

1m / 3ft 1m / 3ft

SUMMER PLANTING

*I*T HAS BEEN *a privilege to share with Ambassador Anne Cox Chambers in the recent evolution of her garden at Le Petit Fontanille in Provence. The haunting scents of pine trees, euphorbias, lavender, thyme, cistus and broom surround Le Petit Fontanille and combine to make it a haven of peace.*

Peter Coats was the guiding light when Anne first arrived in the south of France. He devised for her a garden which merges perfectly into the hills, the woods and olive groves of the surrounding countryside, and yet has great sophistication. Its success lies in combining a profusion of native plants with exotics that are compatible with the climate.

Penstemon 'Sour Grapes' should be treated as half-hardy. Take cuttings in the autumn for next year.

Le Petit Fontanille is extensive enough to have definite areas – the rose garden, the olive grove, the wild flower and lavender fields, the dry bank with native shrubs, the swimming pool garden, all coordinated by the dramatic spires of cypresses and round-headed pines.

A little way from the main garden, beyond a path lined with rosemary bushes, there was an almost flat area. Here was the ideal space for a garden to provide vegetables and flowers for the house. Ryan Gainey designed Anne's potager, and I was asked to plan her cutting garden, with flowers to supplement the evergreens and flowering shrubs to be picked from the main garden.

The space for the cutting garden was 10 × 17m (33 × 55ft). For ease of cutting the beds need to be narrow, with intersecting paths, and I found exactly the design I wanted in a seventeenth-century book, *The English Gardner* by Leonard Meager. I was able to leave the detail of the planting

to Anne's gardener, but I wrote to him with some suggestions.

These are the plants I suggest – I leave you to plant them as you think best.

ANNUALS AND BIENNIALS
Nigella, cleome, verbena, rudbeckia, larkspur, clarkia, sweet williams, scabious, linaria, zinnias, lavatera, asters, antirrhinums and foxgloves.

PERENNIALS
Shasta daisies, dahlias, nepeta, hostas, aquilegias, penstemon, monarda, campanula, *Anthemis tinctoria*, scabious. A selection of roses to match the curtains in the rooms.

You will be able to pick evergreen and other leaves and most roses from other areas of the garden, and I think it best if you concentrate on the above in this garden. It is important when you choose varieties (1) that Ambassador Cox Chambers approves the colours and (2) that they co-ordinate with the colours in the house.

Left: *One of the best forms of golden marguerite,* Anthemis tinctoria *'E.C. Buxton'. The flowers bloom from midsummer through to the first frost and last well in water. It is wise to root a few new basal shoots, because sometimes it will flower itself to death.*

Right: *Among annuals,* Clarkia elegans *is easy from seed and good for picking, the new buds opening as the old flowers fade. Sow a succession of seed.*

Below: *A view across the cutting garden. Beyond are the potager, the meadow and the hillside.*

AN ORNAMENTAL VEGETABLE GARDEN

ANYONE WHO HAS *a love of plants both ornamental and useful, combined with enthusiasm and a definite gastronomic penchant, will derive great satisfaction from the creation of a decorative potager. Here in their garden at the Old Rectory, Sudborough, Northamptonshire, Annie and Tony Huntington decided that they would like an inspiring vegetable garden, one they would enjoy walking through, watching the peas and beans swelling, the salad crops maturing and the fruit ripening.*

The gate opening from the stable yard on the north side is framed by Rosa longicuspis. *Looking through into the potager, you catch a glimpse of the exuberant planting of vegetables and flowers beyond.*

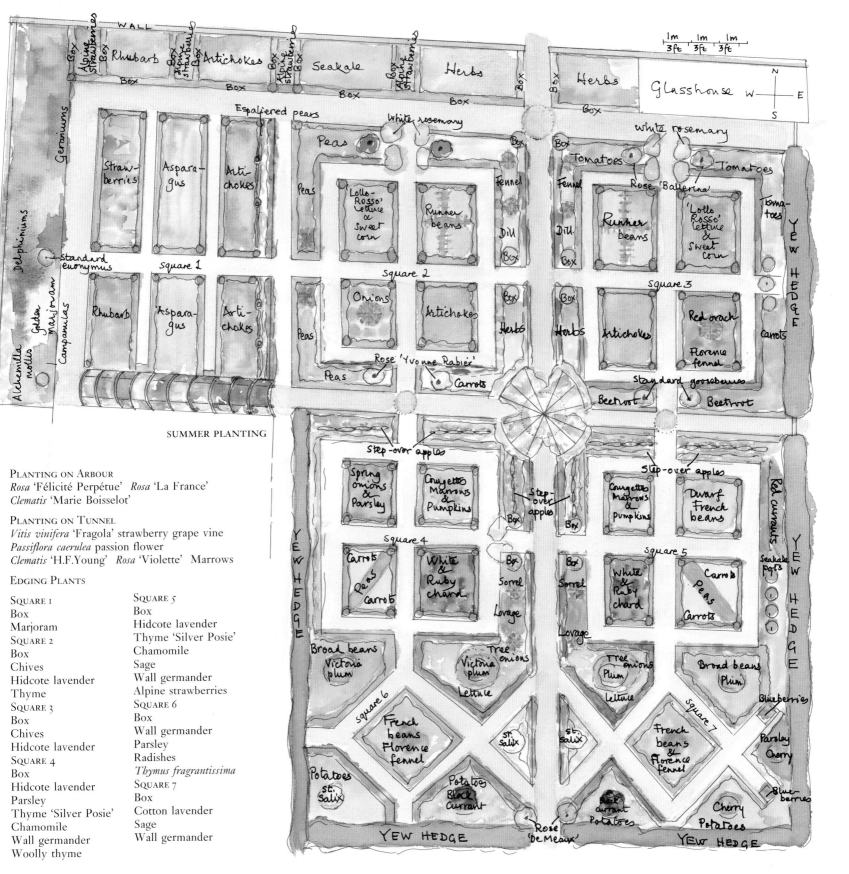

SUMMER PLANTING

PLANTING ON ARBOUR
Rosa 'Félicité Perpétue' *Rosa* 'La France'
Clematis 'Marie Boisselot'

PLANTING ON TUNNEL
Vitis vinifera 'Fragola' strawberry grape vine
Passiflora caerulea passion flower
Clematis 'H.F.Young' *Rosa* 'Violette' Marrows

EDGING PLANTS

SQUARE 1
Box
Marjoram
SQUARE 2
Box
Chives
Hidcote lavender
Thyme
SQUARE 3
Box
Chives
Hidcote lavender
SQUARE 4
Box
Hidcote lavender
Parsley
Thyme 'Silver Posie'
Chamomile
Wall germander
Woolly thyme

SQUARE 5
Box
Hidcote lavender
Thyme 'Silver Posie'
Chamomile
Sage
Wall germander
Alpine strawberries
SQUARE 6
Box
Wall germander
Parsley
Radishes
Thymus fragrantissima
SQUARE 7
Box
Cotton lavender
Sage
Wall germander

III

The Huntingtons had been developing their flower garden for several years, making a rose garden, borders with mixed planting and a successful 'natural' pond. They then turned their minds to the vegetable garden, which had two intersecting paths and no special features. One day they saw my own formally laid out potager, and they invited me to Sudborough to help them.

The existing vegetable patch was bounded on the north side by a red brick wall which the two gardeners, Richard and Robert, were in the throes of repairing. Against it there was an old lean-to glasshouse. The main entrance into this area is through the wall, but you can see from the plan that the path running from it, north to south, is not quite at right angles to the wall. The first major decision was whether to leave this path as it is or to realign it. It had obviously been there for many years, and we found by excavating that it had a considerable depth of hardcore under the gravel. On paper the line looks worrying, but we decided that by the time the box edging and other permanent plants had grown the path's eccentricity would be unnoticeable. Now, five years later, this has proved right. Another important reason for not changing it is that, looking from the south end, it is aligned through the gate on to the church tower. We also kept the cross path, and as this is parallel to the wall the intersection of the two paths is not at right angles. This we successfully disguised by designing a circle of bricks with a rose-covered arbour over the top.

Both for protection and to make a satisfying design the whole area must be enclosed, and I decided that the ideal solution would be yew hedging. We needed 50m (55 yards), which could have been expensive, but by looking around we found

Walk down the path. Standard and climbing roses and bamboo pyramids, later covered by runner beans and sweet peas, add the important dimension of height.

Left: *Near the centre of the potager, standard roses 'Yvonne Rabier', in full flower at midsummer, punctuate the corners of two box-edged beds. In the foreground bed, 'step-over' espaliered apples and thyme 'Silver Posie', interplanted with chamomile, follow the line of the box.*

Right: *In a spring picture of the garden, before it acquires its summer and autumn plumage, the network of box stands out, emphasizing the strong formal design of the beds. The step-over apples are already in blossom.*

Far right: *In late summer, lavender in flower, scarlet runner beans and ripening apples combine to create a picture of joyous exuberance.*

some wonderful plants, 1.2m (4ft) high and reasonably priced – a relief for me as well as for the owners. Now we could turn our attention to planning the patterns of the paths and ordering the bricks.

From practical experience I know that, if space allows, the main paths within a potager should be at least 1m (39in) wide, both for the sake of appearance and for ease of access with wheelbarrows. The subsidiary paths can be narrower. The beds themselves should ideally not be wider than 1.8m (6ft), so that planting and picking is easy. William Lawson, the early-seventeenth-century clergyman gardener and author of *The Country Housewife's Garden*, advised that beds should be narrow, so that the 'weeder women' need not tread on them. We can only repeat the advice Lawson gave his lady parishioners. (Indeed, our vogue for raised beds and minimal digging echoes the same principle.) Equally long-recognized, but often forgotten, is the wisdom of having an edging around each bed. Box at only a few

inches will help to break the cold wind and add a slight protection for young vegetable seedlings. We have noticed the advantage box edging affords in our potager at Barnsley. Young carrots and lettuce are much happier with this slight windbreak.

A permanent feature running from east to west on one side of the central arbour is a metal-framed tunnel. My original proposal was that a mixture of flowers, fruit and vegetables should be grown here, the planting being changed somewhat every year. In the event, the Huntingtons initially planted roses.

My first visit gave me a general impression and after my next visit I sent Annie a proposed overall plan – with plenty of advice! Here are some of my thoughts.

No planting can be done until the paths are laid, and as Richard and Robert will be doing this I recommend that they study the plan carefully before starting.

The pattern of the beds will be defined with box, parsley, alpine

Above: *A view across the clear lines of paths and box-edged beds to the central ornamental arbour. After five years it is completely clad, mostly by rose 'Félicité Perpétue'. The old glasshouse, tactfully restored as a working house, links this modern vegetable garden with times gone by.*

Right: *Looking up the main axis of the potager, past indigo-blue Hidcote lavender and half-standard* Salix integra *'Hakuro-nishiki' to the arbour. The view is framed by a rustic arch of rose 'Rambling Rector', part of the rose tunnel on the south perimeter of the vegetable garden.*

Opposite, left: *Looking the other way. Paths are a lively element in any garden design. Here, three colours of paving material are juxtaposed with the dark lavender, and lead away into a cool grass walk towards the stream and open country beyond.*

Right: *Ironwork has been used extensively in the garden, to provide support for climbers and add interest to different views. The gate and decorative arch shown here are on the eastern edge of the potager.*

strawberries, chives and lavender. For all-the-year-round permanent height, box balls and pyramids, standard roses and gooseberries, fan-trained cherries and apples will be the chief vertical features. From spring through to autumn peas and beans growing through the bamboo frameworks will create height. Consider where these will be used and plan a crop rotation so that after a plentiful manuring peas and beans will be followed by brassicas and then root vegetables.

As your ideas become more sophisticated so you will think up leaf contrasts, feathery carrot tops beside spinach and lettuce, even dark tulips between pale green early lettuces.

Peas and beans can be sown diagonally in the square and rectangular beds, always infilling with the versatile salad crops Remember to use different short-term crops with those which take longer to mature. We interplant cauliflowers with seedling lettuce. These latter will be harvested long before the cauliflowers are ready.

I watched the garden coming on for a year and then handed on my responsibilities to Rupert Golby, who was able to go to Sudborough more often than I could. He lives much closer – and I know that his ideas are along the same lines as mine, so there has not been any conflict of thought. Rupert has brought in many fresh and successful ideas and plenty of enthusiasm. Behind the yew hedge on the south boundary there was a rickety old rose trellis,

Above and right: *In the border under the west wall vegetables give way to flowers, mostly intended for cutting. Tall spires of delphiniums blend with hardy geraniums,* Alchemilla mollis, *golden marjoram and* Campanula persicifolia. *The encrusted stone vase acts as a focal point at the end of the path running under the rose tunnel.*

and when the brick paths at this end of the garden were laid out and the beds planted, the trellis became more prominent and more of an eyesore. The Huntingtons had the good idea of replacing the trellis with another tunnel. The mature roses were gently untied from the trellis and retrained on to the new arches. This took care of one side, and the roses growing up the original tunnel were dug up and replanted on the other side. The new tunnel now provides a backdrop to the potager as well as a scented summer walk. A bonus for me was that my original tunnel could then return to its intended purpose! It now has a vine, clematis and marrows, underplanted with violas, alliums and dianthus.

Annie, being American, knows about pumpkins and blueberries. Both are highly successful at Sudborough. The pumpkin plants are trained up wigwams of bamboos in the centre of one of the squares, the heavy fruit supported in nets. The blueberries, planted in large pots of acid soil, provide focal points at the ends of the diagonal paths. They flowered and fruited abundantly in their first year. It is interesting that they seem to like having their roots confined. They have done much better than some good specimens I put into well-manured ground in another garden a year ago. These have made much new growth but produced no flowers or fruit.

An excellent thing that Rupert has done is to redesign the 2.5m (8ft) deep border at the base of the north wall. He has used box edging to divide it into sections, filling each with a different planting. There are artichokes, seakale and rhubarb, all perennials and permanent, and – on each side of the gate – a useful selection of herbs.

Now (in 1993) this garden is coming up for its sixth year. It is most satisfactory to watch as it develops.

The rose tunnel at the west end of the potager.

BORDER PLANTING, SUMMER

BED 5
White wisteria
Eupatorium rugosum
Honeysuckle
White mallows
Pyrethropsis hosmariensis
Solanum jasminoïdes 'Album'
Hydrangea arborescens 'Annabelle'
Clematis 'Marie Boisselot'
White delphiniums
White daffodils

BED 6
Rosa 'Madame Alfred Carrière'
White delphiniums
White daffodils
Hydrangea arborescens 'Annabelle'
White mallows
Sidalcea
Asters
Garrya elliptica

BED 7
Garrya elliptica
Japanese anemones
White agapanthus
Ilex aquifolium 'Handsworth New Silver'
Dwarf white phlox
Clematis 'Marie Boisselot'
White delphiniums
Aster 'Snow Cushion'
Dicentra formosa alba
Standard *Viburnum × burkwoodii*
Heuchera 'Palace Purple'

BED 8
Standard *Viburnum × burkwoodii*
Heuchera 'Palace Purple'
Clematis 'Marie Boisselot'
Helleborus niger
White agapanthus
Variegated holly
Chaenomeles speciosa 'Nivalis'
Paeonia 'Duchesse de Nemours'
Variegated holly

BED 9
Variegated holly
Osmanthus × burkwoodii
Ilex aquifolium 'Myrtifolia' (x 6)
Geranium macrorrhizum
White mallows
Euonymus fortunei 'Emerald 'n' Gold'
  (x 2)
Hebe pinguifolia 'Pagei' (x 2)

BED 10
Ilex aquifolium 'Myrtifolia' (x 6)
Arabis ferdinandi-coburgii (x 3)
Euonymus fortunei 'Emerald 'n' Gold' (x 2)

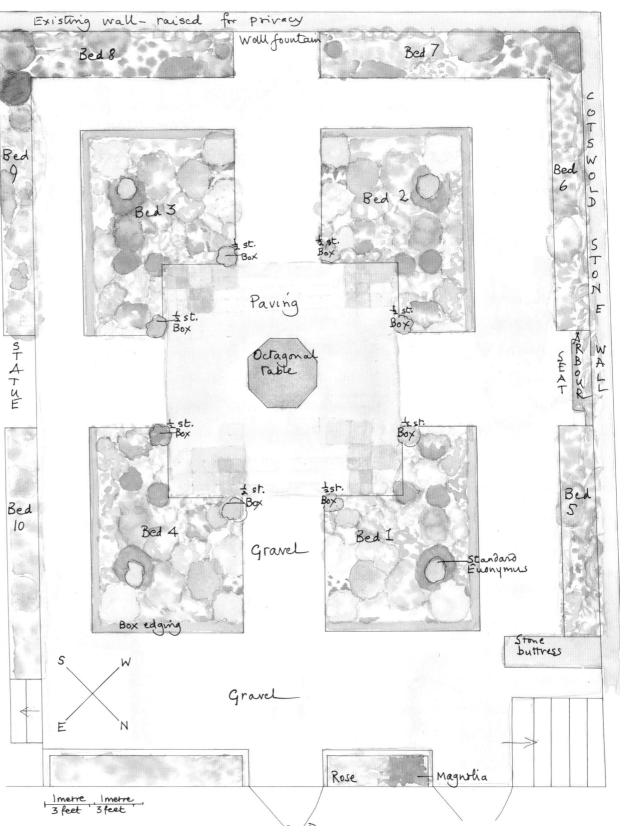

AN OUTDOOR DINING ROOM

*I*T IS MOST *satisfying when a difficult, hitherto wasted area takes on a new and useful role. Outside the dining room windows at Hinton House, in Gloucestershire, was a slope with a bit of a lawn, a few shrubs and a wall which was not high enough to make an effective screen. This rather unexciting space had the potential to be made into a perfect place to sit, drink and dine.*

Hinton House is the home of Reed Cecil and George Cooper. George, while transforming the inside of the house, decided that the south-west-facing windows of the dining room should be replaced by french windows leading into an outdoor living space. This gave Reed the inspiration and the opportunity to make a small garden.

Before any borders could be designed or planting planned, a good deal of hard landscaping had to be undertaken. John Hill and his efficient team came in and levelled the 14 x 10m (46 x 33ft) site. They also raised the height of the wall to create an enclosure. Then together John and I devised the shape for an outdoor dining room. There were to

Above: *The elegant* Penstemon *'White Bedder'. Penstemons are best treated as tender perennials: it is wise to propagate new stock by taking cuttings in autumn, and to overwinter both parent plant and cuttings in a cool glasshouse.*

Right: *Positioned as they are immediately outside the house, and surrounding the outdoor dining area, the L-shaped beds are always a focus of attention, so their planting had to be carefully planned for year-long interest. The neat edging of clipped box, the standard* Euonymus fortunei *'Silver Queen' and the stately foliage of* Yucca flaccida *'Ivory' are as handsome in winter as in summer.* Pulmonaria officinalis *'Sissinghurst White' provides long-lasting ground cover. This summer picture also shows* Viola cornuta alba *(beside* Artemisia *'Powis Castle'),* Scabiosa caucasica *'Miss Willmott',* Tradescantia × andersoniana *'Innocence' and* Penstemon *'White Bedder', all in flower.*

Above: *The eye-catching clover* Trifolium repens *'Purpurascens' will grow from the smallest crack in paving – and a stem with four leaves will bring the finder good luck!*

Left: *A spire of* Yucca flaccida *'Ivory' makes a strong accent. Here it is surrounded by* Penstemon *'White Bedder',* Tradescantia × andersoniana *'Innocence' and* Anthemis punctata *ssp.* cupaniana.

be four L-shaped beds around a central paved area with enough space for an octagonal table and seating for eight people.

At this point the four-year-old *Magnolia grandiflora* 'Exmouth' obligingly flowered and I received an excited telephone call saying 'Let's make this into a white garden.' This seemed an excellent idea, as it would be distracting to have too many colours in this small space, while a green, grey and white planting creates a cool and peaceful atmosphere.

I decided that the four beds should be mirror images of each other and that, apart from a standard euonymus in each bed, all the planting should be kept low. Each bed has dwarf box edging to define the perimeter path, but the planting around the inner edges is allowed to spill out over the paving and gravel to prevent too formal a look.

The beds are filled with white

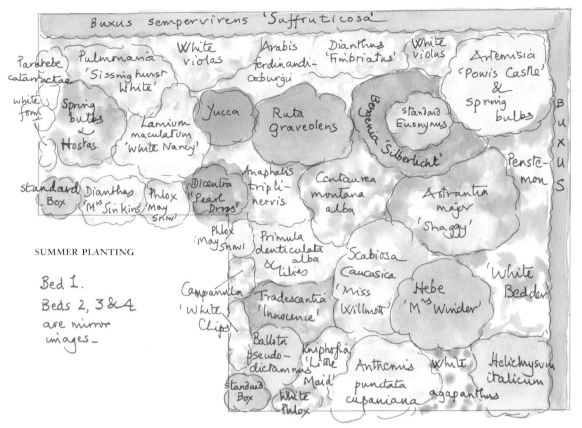

Buxus sempervirens 'Suffruticosa'

Parahebe cataractae / white form / Pulmonaria 'Sissinghurst White' / Spring bulbs & Hostas / White violas / Arabis ferdinandi-coburgii / Lamium maculatum 'White Nancy' / Yucca / Ruta graveolens / Dianthus 'Fimbriatus' / Bergenia 'Silberlicht' / White violas / standard Euonymus / Artemisia 'Powis Castle' & spring bulbs / BUXUS / Penstemon / standard Box / Dianthus 'Mrs Sinkins' / Phlox 'May Snow' / Dicentra 'Pearl Drops' / Anaphalis triplinervis / Centaurea montana alba / Astrantia major 'Shaggy' / Phlox 'May Snow' / Primula denticulata alba & lilies / Scabiosa Caucasica 'Miss Willmott' / Hebe 'Mrs Winder' / 'White Bedder' / Campanula 'White Clips' / Tradescantia 'Innocence' / Ballota pseudo-dictamnus / Kniphofia 'Little Maid' / standard Box / White Phlox / Anthemis punctata cupaniana / agapanthus / White / Helichrysum italicum

SUMMER PLANTING

Bed 1.
Beds 2, 3 & 4 are mirror images.

campanulas, dwarf phlox, dianthus, *Pulmonaria officinalis* 'Sissinghurst White' and, one of my favourite edging plants, the white form of *Parahebe cataractae*. White violas climb through wherever they can. There are generous plantings of hostas, and white crocus and pale narcissus for the spring.

For greys we have rue, *Anthemis punctata* ssp. *cupaniana*, *Artemisia* 'Powis Castle' and *Helichrysum italicum*. The purplish-green leaves of *Hebe* 'Mrs Winder' provide a touch of stronger colour. For silver foliage I chose *Bergenia* 'Silberlicht', but this has not done well and will have to be replaced. Microclimate is something we all need to pay attention to, and we have found out that this seemingly sheltered spot is a frost pocket.

The border around the base of the wall gave the opportunity to introduce more white flowers – delphiniums, mallows, sidalceas, anemones, agapanthus, dicentra and heuchera. Among the climbers, white wisteria and solanum have both proved disappointing. However, *Clematis* 'Marie Boisselot' (syn. *C.* 'Madame le Coultre') and the honeysuckle have done well.

Judith Verity was commissioned to carve a ram's head for a fountain on the wall opposite the french windows, and we put a standard *Viburnum × burkwoodii* on each side to frame it in its focal position.

During the first summer the garden filled out and, thanks to the owners' care, looked well groomed, essential in a small, special place. And I know that as Reed and George discover more white flowers they will introduce them to enrich the planting.

Right: *The green, grey and white theme is represented here by clipped box,* Artemisia *'Powis Castle', white violas and penstemons. The foliage of* Heuchera *'Palace Purple', in the background, provides a darker counterpoint.*

Above: *The pure white grape hyacinth,* Muscari botryoïdes *'Album', flowers in mid-spring. Muscari are excellent for edging and will increase yearly.*

AN ELIZABETHAN GARDEN

*H*OLDENBY HOUSE, *originally built by Sir Christopher Hatton, Queen Elizabeth I's Lord Chancellor, was in its day the largest and most glittering private house in England. At that time, between 1579 and 1587, the gardens were created. We are fortunate that contemporary maps and descriptions enable us to appreciate what this great pleasure garden must have looked like, with its terraces, fish ponds and arches, and the huge flat plateau created by Sir Christopher as the site for a complex knot garden with eight beds.*

In February 1980 James Lowther, who had recently inherited this wonderful house, invited me to Holdenby to consider his project to plant a small Elizabethan garden. Gardens in Elizabethan days were always regular and often geometric. On the west side of the house there was a rectangle of 21 x 27m (23 x 30 yards), enclosed on all sides by yew hedges and walls. Here eight beds had been laid out, a replica in miniature of the shapes of Sir Christopher's great knot garden. James had decided to keep the design of the beds, as this was authentic to the period, but to change the planting.

My brief was twofold. I was to use only plants that were grown in England before 1580, and I was to make the garden as interesting and colourful as possible during

Above: *Red* Erysimum cheiri *brightens the spring border. The ripe seeds are small and light, and easily blown by the wind into wall cracks where they germinate – hence the common name of wallflower.*

Left: *An overall view of the enclosed Elizabethan garden. In the sixteenth century, with fewer flowers available, topiary and patterns were important. Here, box, a shrub indigenous to England, is shaped into square and round forms.*

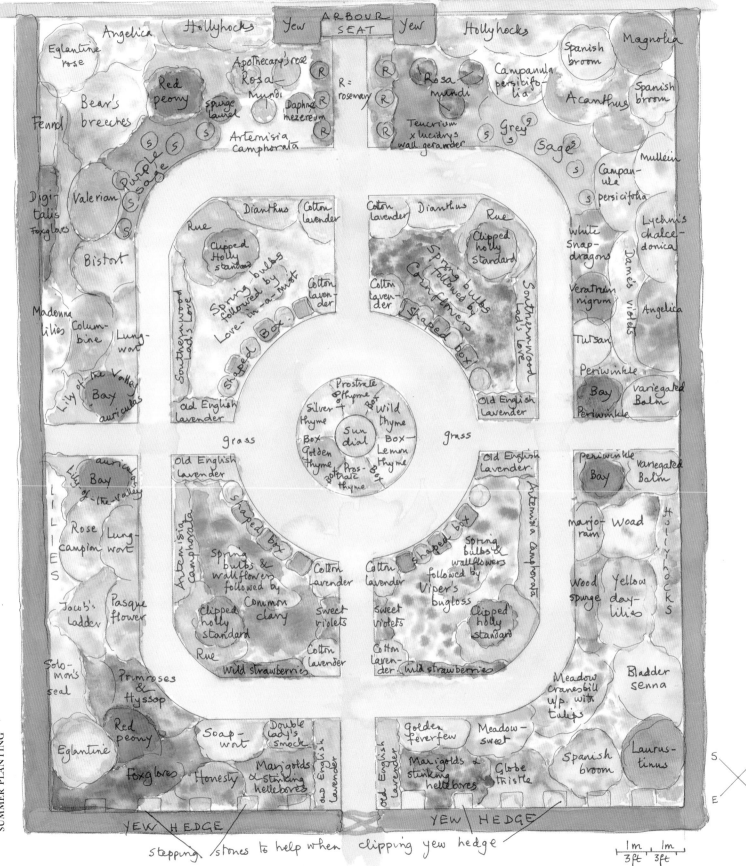

Angelica Hollyhocks **ARBOUR SEAT** Hollyhocks

Yew Yew

Eglantine rose

Apothecary's rose Rosa mundi R R Rosa mundi Spanish broom Magnolia

Red peony Spurge laurel Daphne mezereum R = rosemary R R Campanula persicifolia Spanish broom

Bear's breeches Acanthus

Fennel Artemisia camphorata R R R Teucrium x lucidrys wall germander S Grey S Sage S Mullein

Purple Sage S S S S S S

Digitalis Foxgloves Valerian S Campanula persicifolia S

Bistort

Rue Dianthus Cotton lavender Cotton lavender Dianthus Rue White Snapdragons Lychnis chalcedonica

Clipped Holly standard Clipped holly standard Veratrum nigrum Dames violets

Madonna lilies Columbine Lungwort Southernwood Lad's Love Spring bulbs followed by Love-in-a-Mist Cotton lavender Cotton lavender Spring bulbs followed by Cornflowers Shaped box Southernwood Lad's Love Angelica Tutsan

Shaped Box Periwinkle

Lily of the Valley Bay auriculas Old English Lavender Old English Lavender Bay Periwinkle Variegated Balm

Prostrate thyme

grass Silver thyme Wild thyme grass

Box Sun dial Box

Golden thyme Lemon thyme

Prostrate thyme

auriculas Bay Lily of-the-valley Old English Lavender Old English Lavender Periwinkle Bay Variegated Balm

LILIES Rose campion Lung- wort Artemisia camphorata Shaped box Shaped box Artemisia camphorata marjo- ram Woad Hollyhocks

Jacob's Ladder Pasque Flower Spring bulbs & wallflowers followed by Common clary Cotton Lavender Cotton lavender Spring bulbs & wallflowers followed by Viper's bugloss Wood spurge Yellow day- lilies

Clipped holly standard Sweet violets Sweet violets Clipped holly standard

Rue Cotton Lavender Cotton lavender

Solomon's seal Wild strawberries Wild strawberries Meadow cranesbill up. with tulips Bladder senna

Primroses & Hyssop

Red peony Soap- wort Double Lady's smock Old English Lavender Old English Lavender Golden Feverfew Meadow- sweet Spanish broom Laurus- tinus

Eglantine Foxgloves Honesty Marigolds & stinking hellebores Marigolds & stinking hellebores Globe thistle

YEW HEDGE **YEW HEDGE**

stepping stones to help when clipping yew hedge

S W

E N

1m 3ft 1m 3ft

the months from April until the end of
September, when the house and grounds
are open to the public.

This is where the old writers were
invaluable: Thomas Hyll, William Turner,
John Gerard and Dodoens in the sixteenth
century, William Lawson, John Parkinson
and John Rea in the seventeenth.
Researching the planting was fascinating for
me, as I became increasingly aware of those
plants which are indigenous to England and
others which were introduced very early.
I was particularly struck by colour. There
were blues, many yellows, lots of white,
not many pink flowers, except for roses,
and I can think of few reds that were
generally grown – *Paeonia officinalis,* wallflowers. All the plants had quite recently
been brought in from the wild, so their
foliage was generally green. Most variations
did not occur until later. There were
exceptions, though, among them variegated
hollies, which are mentioned in early records.
Fragrant flowers were loved, and writers
always mentioned scent. Everything I read
reinforced my belief that the sixteenth-
century pleasure garden had plants for
beauty and fragrance as well as medicinal
and salad herbs.

Left: *Annual nigella, love-in-a-mist.*

Below: *Alpine strawberries, brought to England by
the Romans, mix with lucky four-leaved clover
and pulmonaria. Four different varieties of
pulmonaria were mentioned by Gerard in 1597.*

My first suggestion was a practical one. I asked the head gardener to have the beds thoroughly dug and well manured and also to add enough topsoil to raise their level so that they were slightly higher than the grass paths. Luckily the beds were symmetrical and an existing sundial was exactly central, so we had a good start.

In my design, working from the centre outwards, we surrounded the sundial with thymes, five different varieties. The four inner beds have various edgings. Dwarf box shapes delineate their inner edges. On the corners of the cross paths are cotton lavender and old English lavender, both scented in leaf and flower. On the outer edges of these four beds are wild strawberries, rue and dianthus and two different artemisias. *Artemisia abrotanum*, southernwood, is also called lad's love, because, it is said, a decoction of it will make young men's beards grow faster. *A. alba* until recently went by the more descriptive name of *A. camphorata*. Hung in the clothes' cupboard, it will keep moths away.

For spring colour we chose scillas and jonquils, with lots of primroses and cowslips, planted between wallflowers. For summer we have in two of the beds love-in-a-mist (nigella) and cornflowers. By pounding cornflowers in a mortar, artists could obtain a juice to add to alum, providing a vivid blue to incorporate into the oils for their paintings. Blue viper's bugloss and clary sage fill the centres of the other two beds, so there is a general impression of blue.

In the outer beds, taller shrubs provide a background: laurustinus, rosemary, bay and spurge laurel for evergreens, Spanish broom for summer colour, the eglantine rose (sweetbriar), with its scent of ripe apples, and *Rosa gallica* 'Versicolor', the fabled Rosa Mundi, with its striped flowers. Between and around them we have a variety of herbaceous plants – hollyhocks, campanulas, marigolds, foxgloves, primroses, columbines, and more, all plants recommended by the early writers.

History should always go hand in hand with artistic vision when old gardens are being brought back to life. What I would like best is to have the privilege of walking round the garden with Sir Christopher Hatton on one side and James Lowther on the other, learning more about the sixteenth century.

Above: *Gerard wrote that, 'Cowslips and primroses joy in moist and dankish places. They flourish from April to the end of May.'*
Below, left: *Rosa Mundi is a midsummer wonder supposedly named after Fair Rosamund, mistress of King Henry II.*
Below: *In 1551 William Turner wrote, 'Blewbottel groweth in the corn.' Cornflower is a hardy annual.*

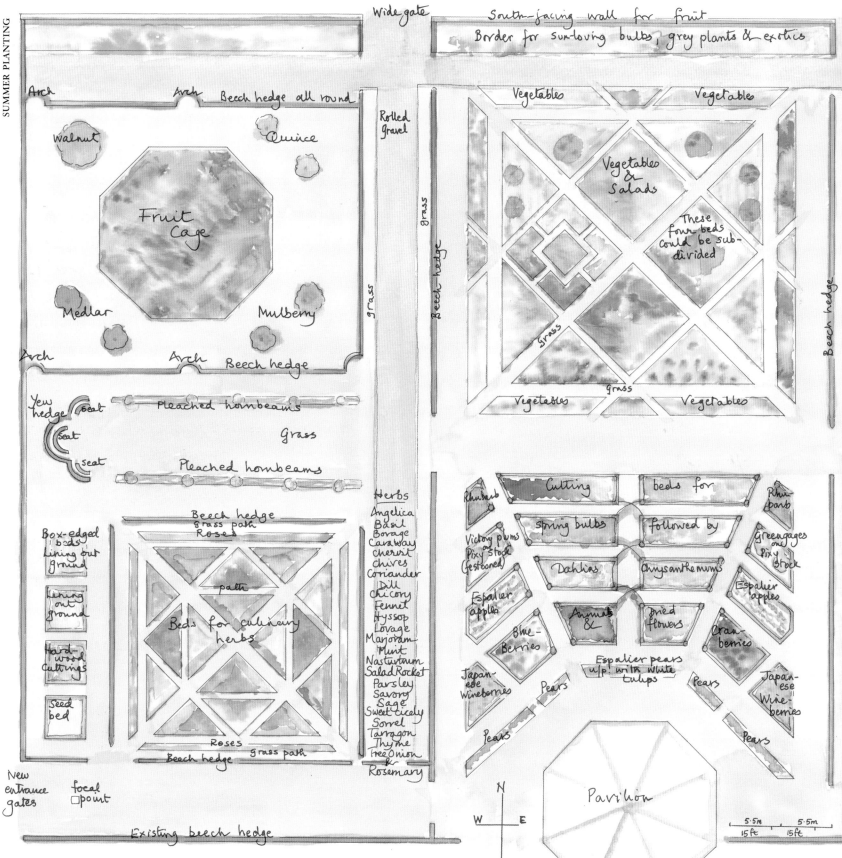

Wide gate

South-facing wall for fruit

Border for sun-loving bulbs, grey plants & exotics

Arch   Arch   Beech hedge all round

Walnut   Quince

Rolled Gravel

grass

Fruit Cage

Vegetables   Vegetable

Vegetables & Salads

These four beds could be sub-divided

grass

grass

Beech hedge

Medlar   Mulberry

Beech hedge

grass

Arch   Arch   Beech hedge

Yew hedge   seat   Pleached hornbeams

seat

seat   Grass

Pleached hornbeams

Vegetables   grass   Vegetables

Herbs

Angelica
Basil
Borage
Caraway
Chervil
Chives
Coriander
Dill
Chicory
Fennel
Hyssop
Lovage
Marjoram
Mint
Nasturtium
Salad Rocket
Parsley
Savory
Sage
Sweet Cicely
Sorrel
Tarragon
Thyme
Tree Onion
&
Rosemary

Rhubarb   Cutting   beds for   Rhubarb

Beech hedge
Grass path
Roses

Box-edged beds
Lining out ground

Spring bulbs   Followed by

Greengages one Pixy stock

Victory plums Pixy stock (festooned)

lining out ground

Dahlias   Chrysanthemums

path

Espalier apples

Espalier apples

Hard-wood cuttings

Beds for culinary herbs

Annuals &   Dried flowers

Blue-Berries

Cran-berries

Seed bed

Japanese Wineberries   Pears   Espalier pears u/p with white tulips   Pears   Japanese Wine berries

Roses
Beech hedge   grass path

Pears   Pears

New entrance gates   focal point

Pavilion

Existing beech hedge

N
W   E
S

5.5m   5.5m
15ft   15ft

128

A PRODUCTIVE POTAGER

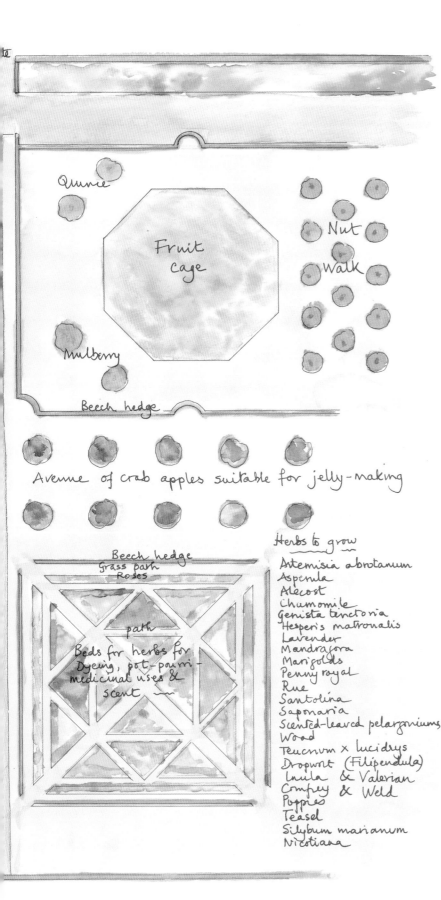

Quince

Fruit cage

Nut Walk

Mulberry

Beech hedge

Avenue of crab apples suitable for jelly-making

Beech hedge
Grass path
Roses

path

Beds for herbs for Dyeing, pot-pourri, medicinal uses & scent

Herbs to grow

Artemisia abrotanum
Asperula
Alecost
Chamomile
Genista tinctoria
Hesperis matronalis
Lavender
Mandragora
Marigolds
Penny royal
Rue
Santolina
Saponaria
Scented-leaved pelargoniums
Woad
Teucrium x lucidrys
Dropwort (Filipendula)
Inula & Valerian
Comfrey & Weld
Poppies
Teasel
Silybum marianum
Nicotiana

MY FIRST ASSOCIATION *with Lord Bute and his garden at Mount Stuart, on the island of Bute, off the west coast of Scotland, came in 1990. The head gardener, Paul Martin, visited me in the autumn of that year to discuss the possibility that I might go to Mount Stuart to plan with him the future of the walled garden. Since then I have been there regularly each spring and autumn.*

John, 6th Marquess of Bute, is a visionary and a patron of the arts, and he has done much to preserve and modernize his amazing Victorian house with its ingenious and dominating William Burges features. The huge mansion is a unique nineteenth-century showpiece, yet at the same time a warm and comfortable home.

In the nineteenth century there was at some distance from the house a large (1.82 ha/4½ acre) vegetable garden capable of growing produce for the needs of the household and staff. My brief was to design for this site a potager that would be decorative and productive and also educational for the thousands of visitors who come to the estate each season.

The existing features were a high brick

wall, 130m (142 yards) long, on the north side, and, on the south side, a new octagonal glass pavilion to grow exotic and tender plants. The north wall was punctuated by two wide gateways recently redesigned by the Edinburgh architect Stewart Tod. There was a fruit cage in the north-west corner and there were also various functional tool and machinery sheds and glasshouses. These were all destined to be re-sited in a new working area beyond the wall.

My thoughts were to divide the large ground between the wall and the pavilion into six well-defined areas. First I attended to the vegetables, which must have top priority. Then I planned two different herb gardens, one for culinary herbs and the other for medicinal, scented and dyeing herbs. I studied the herbals of John Gerard, Parkinson and Culpeper to make sure we had all the right old remedies. A cutting garden would provide flowers for every season, to be supplemented by greenery and flowering shrubs from other parts of the garden. This left me with two spaces for soft fruit. I envisaged decorative octagonal cages (to mirror the pavilion), and Stewart Tod drew up the plans. Look at the drawn-out design and you will see how vistas can be as important in a potager as in a flower garden.

The land on the south side of the pavilion will one day have fruit trees planted in a quincunx – all apples and pears which were grown for their flavour and keeping qualities in the seventeenth and eighteenth centuries.

We will also keep spaces for bees and exotic fowls. The garden must have bee hives nearby to maintain the fruit supply, and hens and ducks are a major attraction for visiting schoolchildren.

The red stems of ruby chard combine with pale green lettuce, to decorative effect.

Sweet peas contribute their delicious fragrance and a wealth of flowers for cutting – the more you cut, the more flowers grow.

Above, left: *Pencil-podded stringless dwarf French beans, easy to pick and excellent for freezing.*
Left: *A globe artichoke ready to eat (on the bottom left), others allowed to produce their handsome flowers. Artichokes can be treated as perennials, but they need winter protection.*

Left: *A fan-trained apple tree, laden with ripening fruit in autumn. Trained in an espalier, fruit trees look delightful and occupy the minimum amount of space.*

Below: *The double-flowered chamomile, Chamaemelum nobile 'Flore Pleno'. One of the most ancient medicinal herbs, chamomile is also used in pot-pourri, and to make a soothing tea.*

SYMMETRY IN A SMALL GARDEN

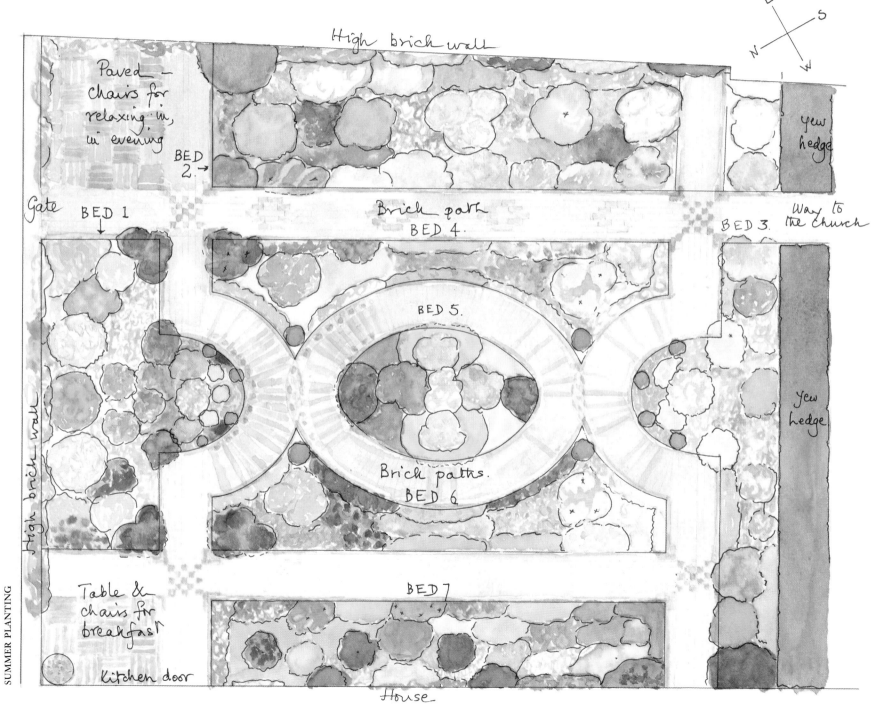

E
S
N
W

High brick wall

Paved — chairs for relaxing in, in evening

Yew hedge

BED 2 →

Gate

BED 1
↓

Brick path
BED 4.

Way to the church

BED 3.

BED 5.

Yew Hedge

Brick paths.
BED 6

Table & chairs for breakfast

BED 7

Kitchen door

House

1 metre
3 feet

IT IS ALWAYS a pleasure for me to design a garden in a small enclosed space where the owners will enjoy sitting, especially when I know that they will also work to keep it pristine and full of year-long interest. Beyond the east wall of the garden at the Old Rectory, Berwick, East Sussex, is a background of mature trees and a beautiful old church.

The paths around the central area are defined by box balls, Santolina chamaecyparissus *and the tidy* Hebe topiaria. *Pink predominates, with* Lavatera *'Barnsley',* Cistus *'Silver Pink' and rose 'Mary Rose'.*

Several windows look out on to the garden but to reach it you had to walk from the front door round to the back of the house, so it had never been fully enjoyed. This is a sheltered site, and I felt that, once it was made more accessible and attractive, Tim and Mary Jones would use the corner facing south-east as a quiet sitting place for breakfast. The south-west-facing corner would be an ideal spot for relaxing in the evening to catch the setting sun. So my first

approach was to persuade the owners to make the existing kitchen window into a door. This immediately positioned the first path, and from this I drew out a symmetrical layout incorporating the view from the window in Tim's study. The relative areas of borders and path had to be carefully considered. It was obviously important to be able to walk around easily, and there must always be enough plant colour and shape to enjoy through the year.

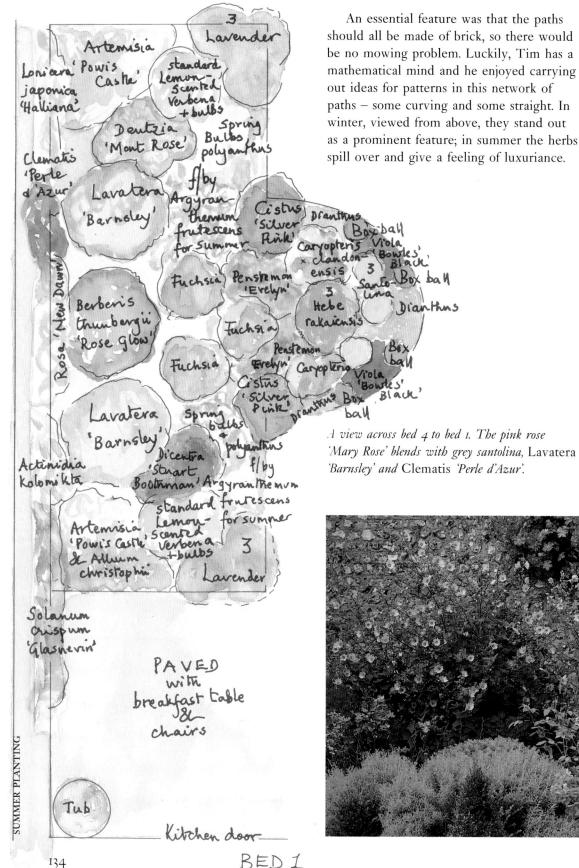

An essential feature was that the paths should all be made of brick, so there would be no mowing problem. Luckily, Tim has a mathematical mind and he enjoyed carrying out ideas for patterns in this network of paths – some curving and some straight. In winter, viewed from above, they stand out as a prominent feature; in summer the herbs spill over and give a feeling of luxuriance.

A view across bed 4 to bed 1. The pink rose 'Mary Rose' blends with grey santolina, Lavatera *'Barnsley' and* Clematis *'Perle d'Azur'.*

As the rest of the Old Rectory garden has a wide variety of trees, shrubs and perennials, I felt that an important part of my role was to introduce plenty of herbs for Mary to use in her imaginative cooking. There must be scented plants too, and a range of flowers and foliage for cutting, starting with spring bulbs and going on to roses and annuals, plants for posies and autumn colour.

In a small area it is important to keep the colours in harmony, and here the scheme fitted into the four different aspects. The west-facing border, which gets the evening sun, is the backdrop seen from the house. I decided that it should have a pink and grey theme, and grey foliage. I planned that the shady east-facing border, under the house, would depend mostly on foliage, and the north-facing border, under the yew hedge, would have shrubs with gold or variegated leaves. The sunny bed between the two sitting areas would have scented plants in pale and dark pinks, grey and mauve. The plants in the central beds should be low, scented and useful in the kitchen.

Left: *In spring the midday sun lights up the golden foliage of* Lonicera nitida *'Baggesen's Gold', clipped into pyramids, in bed 3. Their colour echoes the chartreuse-yellow of* Euphorbia polychroma's *flowers. In shape they provide a contrast to the rounded forms of* Hebe rakaiensis *and the box balls.*

Below: *Deep pink* Penstemon *'Evelyn', one of the hardiest penstemons, contributes to the rich summer colour of Bed 1.*

The south-facing border (bed 1) is designed to be luxuriant through the warm months when Mary and Tim and their guests sit out in the garden. It is closely planted for scent, colour and evolving interest. Structure is achieved using clipped box balls, lavender, *Hebe rakaiensis* and standard verbenas; polyanthus and spring bulbs are important too. On the brick wall behind, roses, clematis, honeysuckle, the potato vine and *Actinidia kolomikta* thrive, enjoying this sunny site.

The north-facing border (bed 3), under the yew hedge, was more of a problem to fill. The structure was created by box balls to match those in the south bed, and by evergreens – euonymus, hebe, *Lonicera nitida* 'Baggesen's Gold' (clipped!), variegated rhamnus, euphorbia, bergenia and choisya. This did not leave much space for flower colour, but acanthus, *Lysimachia ephemerum*, pulmonaria and Solomon's seal were incorporated. Bulbs were planted for spring interest, followed by nicotianas.

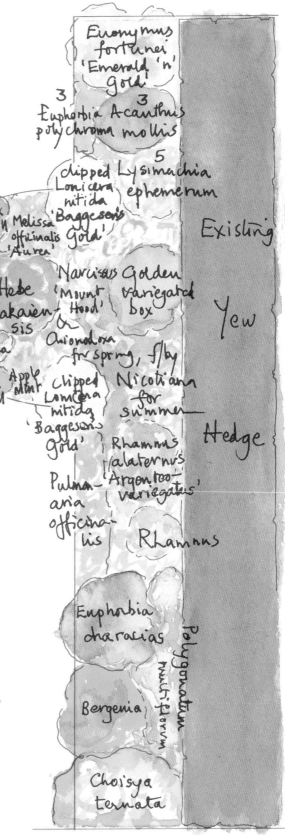

BED 3

SUMMER PLANTING

Osmanthus x burkwoodii
clematis 'Comtesse de Bouchaud'
Rosa 'compassion'
clematis 'Jackmanii superba'
Rosa 'Highfield'
Ceanoth 'Puget Bl

5 Verbascum phoeniceum
Philadelphus 'Belle Etoile'
5 Campanula 'Loddon Anna'
Pink hollyhock
7 Special Dark Purple Honesty
= 7 Lunaria annua

Scented-leaved pelargoniums & Violas

Viburnum plicatum 'Mariesii'
Monarda (Bergamot)
Kolkwitzia amabilis
7 Digitalis grandiflora
3 Rosa 'Emannel' (pale pink)
5 Veronicastrum virginicum
Spiraea 'Arguta'
7 Verbascum phoeniceum
Escallonia 'Iveyi'

Spring bulbs & hostas
9 Crocosmia 'Solfaterre'

9 Penstemon 'Rich Ruby'
3 Rosemary
Caryopteris x clandonensis
5 Stachys byzantina
7 Erysimum 'Bowles' Mauve'
Anthemis punctata cupaniana
5 Anaphalis margaritacea cinnamomea
Hemerocallis 'Stella de Oro'
Spiraea japonica 'Gold flame' & violas

BED 2. →

SUMMER PLANTING

The elegant, arching stems of Solomon's seal bear hanging white flowers in summer.

The new fronds of Matteuccia struthiopteris *unfurl in spring to form a beautiful foliage vase.*

The handsome Hosta sieboldiana *var.* elegans. *I like to group hostas, for a bold effect.*

SPRING PLANTING

Saxifraga x urbium 'Aureopunctata = variegata London Pride x 11
7 Vinca minor alba
3 Hosta
5 Tiarella cordifolia
5 Helleborus orientalis
7 Vinca minor - blue
7 Tolmiea menziesii
3 Helleborus orientalis
Bergenia

Ferns
Ferns
Ferns
Bergenia
Euphorbia cyparissias
Epimedium
Hosta 3
Harts tongue fern 3
Bronze fennel

Skimmia japonica reevesiana
Buxus sempervirens 'Aureovariegata'
Choisya ternata
Choisya ternata
7 Aquilegia
7 Hesperis matronalis
7 Helleborus argutifolius

Lily of the Valley
Helleborus foetidus
fennel
5 Fennel
5 Polygonatum multiflorum
3 Digitalis
3 Helleborus foetidus
Cotoneaster conspicuus 'Decorus'

BED 7
Clematis tangutica
Jasminum — nudiflorum — Jasminum
Jasminum
Pyracantha atalantioides.

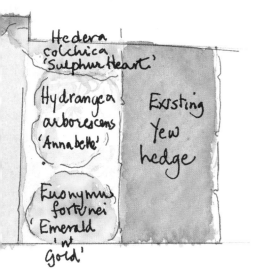

Hedera
colchica
'Sulphur Heart'

Hydrangea
arborescens
'Annabelle'

Existing
Yew
hedge

Euonymus
fortunei
'Emerald
'n'
Gold'

Below: *The iron statue, once painted white, now become rusty, has just the right character to combine with the brick and flint wall behind. The paving has also mellowed. Violas and variegated euonymus emphasize the corners of bed 2.*

Above: *In late summer and autumn, bed 2 is predominantly green and white, with occasional splashes of rich colour. At the end near the gate the magnificent flower panicles of* Hydrangea arborescens *'Annabelle' stand out against the dark trelliswork.*

The important west-facing border (bed 2) is planted especially for spring and autumn. The wall has late-flowering clematis and roses in pink and white, with deep purple *Clematis* 'Jackmanii Superba' and *Ceanothus* 'Puget Blue' for colour contrast. There is a backbone of shrubs, osmanthus, *Viburnum plicatum* 'Mariesii' – its dramatic shape providing emphasis at the end of the border – philadelphus, kolkwitzia, spiraea and *Escallonia* 'Iveyi'. These are infilled with hardy and half-hardy perennials and a few biennials. Of course there must be spring bulbs – narcissus and tulips – and these are followed by hostas and scented pelargoniums.

The east-facing border (bed 7), under the house wall, is dry and rather sunless. It is surprising how many plants will survive in these conditions, but most of them have sober colours or are predominantly green. I have chosen *Clematis tangutica, Jasminum nudiflorum,* pyracantha and cotoneaster for the house wall. There are lots of hellebores and ferns, hostas and periwinkles. Epimediums, tiarella and tolmiea keep the ground well clothed in winter, and will flower in spring.

The oval-shaped central bed (5) has plenty of parsley, sage, sweet cicely and marjoram, with curry plant and rue for extra scent.

The two embracing beds (4 and 6) unite the colour scheme used in the four outside borders. They are pink, changing to yellow – the pink rose 'Mary Rose' at one end, and the yellow rose 'Graham Thomas' at the other. To keep a succession of colour there are spring bulbs followed by tender diascias, felicias and scented-leaved pelargoniums.

These beds are edged with chives, wall germander *(Teucrium × lucidrys)* and *Epilobium glabellum*. The curve at one end is emphasized by the grey-leaved *Hebe topiaria*, and that at the other by low-growing variegated euonymus. I put box pyramids on the four acute points of the borders, to make sure that neither people nor animals will trespass on them.

The sweetly scented pink rose 'Mary Rose', raised by David Austin, was named for Henry VIII's flagship. I had originally planned to use the David Austin roses 'Wife of Bath' and 'Pretty Jessica' in beds 4 and 6, but when they were not available we substituted 'Mary Rose'.

Left: *The old wall in the north-east corner is now well clothed with rose 'Climbing Iceberg' and* Clematis montana *var.* rubens, *growing from the north side and enjoying the south aspect. The pretty iron seat and wooden table show appropriate signs of age.*

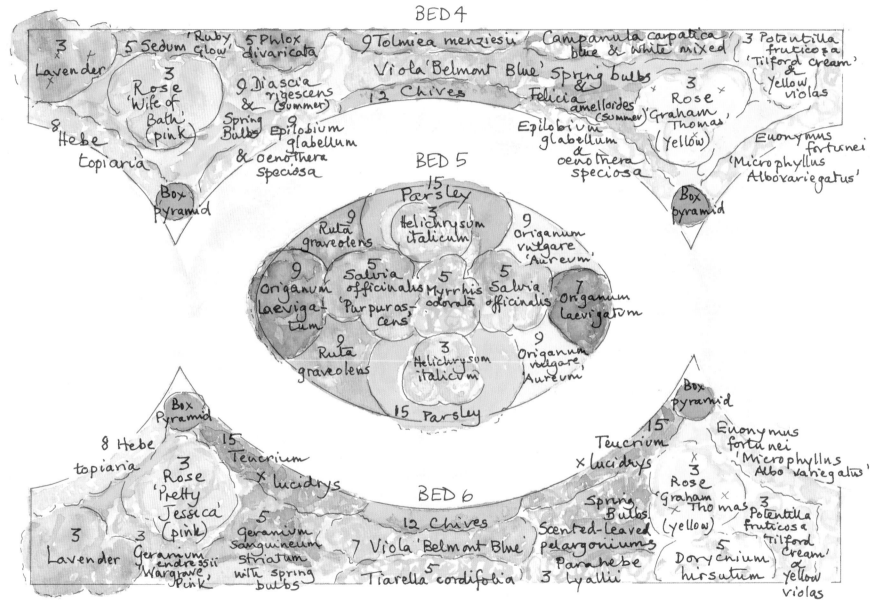

BED 4

3 Lavender

5 Sedum 'Ruby Glow'

5 Phlox divaricata

9 Tolmiea menziesii

Campanula carpatica blue & white mixed

3 Potentilla fruticosa 'Tilford Cream'

3 Rose 'Wife of Bath' (pink)

9 Diascia rigescens & (summer)

Viola 'Belmont Blue' Spring bulbs &

Yellow violas

8 Hebe topiaria

12 Chives

Felicia amelloides (summer)

3 Rose 'Graham Thomas' (Yellow)

Spring Bulbs

9 Epilobium glabellum & oenothera speciosa

Epilobium glabellum & oenothera speciosa

Euonymus fortunei 'Microphyllus Alboxariegatus'

Box pyramid

Box pyramid

BED 5

15 Parsley

9 Ruta graveolens

3 Helichrysum italicum

9 Origanum vulgare 'Aureum'

9 Origanum laevigatum

5 Salvia officinalis Purpurascens

5 Myrrhis odorata

5 Salvia officinalis

7 Origanum laevigatum

9 Ruta graveolens

3 Helichrysum italicum

9 Origanum vulgare 'Aureum'

15 Parsley

Box pyramid

8 Hebe topiaria

Box Pyramid

15 Teucrium × lucidrys

15 Teucrium × lucidrys

Euonymus fortunei 'Microphyllus Albo variegatus'

3 Rose 'Pretty Jessica' (pink)

BED 6

Spring Bulbs

3 Rose 'Graham × Thomas' (yellow)

3 Potentilla fruticosa 'Tilford Cream'

3 Lavender

3 Geranium endressii 'Wargrave Pink'

5 Geranium sanguineum striatum with spring bulbs

12 Chives

7 Viola 'Belmont Blue'

Scented-leaved pelargoniums

5 Dorycnium hirsutum

Yellow violas

5 Tiarella cordifolia

Parahebe 3 Lyallii

SUMMER PLANTING

Left: *Looking from the north end of bed 6, towards bed 3 in the distance. In the foreground,* 'Mary Rose' *and* Geranium × oxonianum 'Wargrave Pink' *flower in a harmony of pink.*

ROSEMARY VEREY'S GARDEN PLANS:
A COMPLETE LIST

Ablington Manor, Gloucestershire, 1983
Walled garden for Robert Cooper

Ascott Place, Berkshire, 1989
Old walled garden

Atlanta, Georgia, 1984
General designing for Richard Lewis

Barnsley House, Gloucestershire, 1950 onwards
Garden design and planting

Bourton-in-the-Water, Gloucestershire
An enclosed herb garden

Buckhurst Park, Berkshire, 1991
General advice

Burford, Oxfordshire
Garden design and planting for Lord Windlesham

Chapter Manor, Gloucestershire, 1988
Knot garden for Lord Fanshawe

The Chelsea Flower Show, London, 1992
A small town garden

Cirencester, Gloucestershire, 1993
*A small town garden for Rev. and
Mrs Francis Bruce*

Colnpen House, Gloucestershire
*Herb border and general planting for Mr and
Mrs Rupert Watson*

Fort Belvedere, Berkshire, 1983
*Borders and a rose garden for Mr and Mrs
Galen Weston*

The Garden Club of Jacksonville, Florida, 1990
Knot garden

Glebe House, Bibury, Gloucestershire
*General planning and planting for
Douglas McMillan*

Halls Grove, Gloucestershire, 1990
Border planting for Mr and Mrs Peter Gibbs

Hammerton House, Gloucestershire
*Parterre beds and planting around pool for
Anne Norman*

Highgrove House, Gloucestershire
*Planting plans for 'cottage garden', long
raised beds, and woodland underplanting for
HRH the Prince of Wales*

Hinton House, Gloucestershire, 1991
White garden for Reed Cecil and George Cooper

Holdenby House, Northamptonshire, 1980
*Elizabethan garden and scented borders for
James Lowther*

Ivy House, Wiltshire
Border designs for Mrs Pedersen

Kilkenny Farm, Gloucestershire
*Border planting around pool for
Mrs John Phillips*

Lime Close, Oxfordshire, 1992
*A herb garden for Prince Pierre d'Arenberg and
Marie-Christine de Laubarède*

The Little House, Barnsley,
Gloucestershire, 1984
*Entrance, parterre beds, potager and general border
planting for Mr and Mrs Arthur Reynolds*

The Little House Farmhouse, Barnsley,
Gloucestershire, 1989
Garden design for Mr and Mrs Arthur Reynolds

Longleat House, Wiltshire, 1985
*Herbaceous borders for the late Marquess and
the Marchioness of Bath*

Luton Hoo, Bedfordshire
Scented garden for the late Hon. Nicholas Phillips

The Montreal International Floralies, 1980
A herb garden

Mount Stuart, Isle of Bute, 1990 onwards
Potager for the Marquess of Bute

Nether Lypiatt Manor, Gloucestershire, 1987
*A raised flower bed and the herb garden for
Princess Michael of Kent*

Notgrove Manor, Gloucestershire
Border planting for Mrs David Acland

The Old Rectory, Berwick, East Sussex, 1990
Garden design for Mr and Mrs Tim Jones

The Old Rectory, Sudborough,
Northamptonshire, 1988
Potager for Mr and Mrs Anthony Huntington

Orchard Farm House, Gloucestershire, 1985
Knot garden for the Misses Barrie

Le Petit Fontanille, Provence, 1990
Cutting garden for Ambassador Anne Cox Chambers

Rectory Farm, Turkdean, Gloucestershire
Planting around pool for Annie Daniels

Somerford Keynes House, Wiltshire
*Garden design and planting for Sir Theodore
and Lady Brinckman*

Sudeley Castle, Gloucestershire
Border design for Lady Ashcombe

Sundridge Park, Bromley, Kent, 1992
Herbaceous borders for Sundridge Park Management

Williamstrip Park, Gloucestershire
Vegetable garden for the late Earl St Aldwyn

Woodside, Berkshire, 1989 onwards
*White garden, scented garden, herbaceous borders,
potager, woodland planting for Elton John*

INDEX

ACKNOWLEDGMENTS

AUTHOR'S ACKNOWLEDGMENTS

I wish to acknowledge the help and inspiration given me by many people over the years. I especially thank Frances Lincoln and Erica Hunningher, who suggested the idea for this book; Jo Christian, who has been tactful and patient with me throughout while compiling the chapters; Jean Sturgis, whose skill at painting has brought my drawings to life; Tony Lord, for his assistance with plant names; Andrew Lawson, Jerry Harpur, Mick Hales and the other photographers for their skill; all the owners of the gardens for allowing me to use the plans; Katherine Lambert for deciphering my handwriting.

My grateful thanks for the special help given me in designing and creating the Chelsea 1992 garden by John Hill and his team, Diana Reynell, Rupert Golby, Hughie Powell, Simon Verity, Derek Elliott, and Recollections, Ltd. Thanks also to Gordon Taylor and Guy Cooper, my co-designers at Woodside; and to Helen Finch (née Greenwood), head gardener at Woodside, and her team of helpers. Also to Michael Balston; Dick Balfour; Tony at Fort Belvedere; Carol Newman; Margie Trevelyan Clark; and Anne Norman, who persuaded me to hold a year of gardening classes which taught me much about the basics of gardening.

It is a privilege to work and discuss plans with other designers. Both Tim Rees and Rupert Golby have been generous with their creative thoughts. I will always be grateful to my own gardeners, Andy and Leslie Bailey, who are enthusiastic and full of ideas. I thank my son, Charles Verey, for allowing me to continue caring for the garden at Barnsley House.

PHOTOGRAPHIC ACKNOWLEDGMENTS

a = above, b = below, c = centre, l = left, r = right
All photographs copyright © Andrew Lawson, except for the following:
Deni Bown: 103*bl*, 103*bc*
Geoff Dann © FLL: 136*r*
Mick Hales: 109*b*
Jerry Harpur: 86, 89, 110, 112-13, 114, 116, 117, 118, 119
Andrew Lawson © FLL: 19*r*, 49*l*, 50, 54*ar*, 72*a*, 77*bc*, 103*br*
Tony Lord: 6-7, 12-13, 14*a*, 17
S. & O. Mathews: 133, 134, 137*a*
Steve Wooster © FLL: 25*r* (Beth Chatto), 77*ar* (Beth Chatto)

PUBLISHERS' ACKNOWLEDGMENTS

The publishers wish to thank Sally Cracknell, for invaluable assistance with the artwork; and Hilary Hockman, Annabel Morgan and Caroline Taylor, for editorial help.

Design by Studio Gossett

Horticultural consultant Tony Lord
Editor Jo Christian
Art Editor Louise Tucker
Picture Editor Anne Fraser
Indexer Penny David
Production Annemarieke Kroon

Editorial Director Erica Hunningher
Art Director Caroline Hillier
Production Director Nicky Bowden